MASTERING BUSINESS FOR STRATEGIC COMMUNICATORS

Insights and Advice from the
C-suite of Leading Brands

Mastering Business for Strategic Communicators is a gem and a must-read for anyone aspiring to lead communications for any organization. It makes clear that to be a top communicator today you have to be a business leader first, mine data and relationships, and find ways to transform strategy into relationships and results.

— *Mike Fernandez, Chief Executive Officer,*
U.S., Burson-Marsteller

Matt and Ron are on a mission: To make sure PR's next generation is schooled in the foundations of business and thus regularly asked into the "room where it happens." Through chapters contributed by many of today's most successful communicators, along with observations by leading C-suite executives, their newest book will go a long way towards helping students — as well as those building careers — easily and more fully understand business at the intersection of strategic communications. I used their first book in my classroom at Boston University. I will use their new one, too.

— *Ray Kotcher, Professor of the Practice,*
Boston University College of Communication
and Non-Executive Chairman, Ketchum

Wow! What an outstanding read! Featuring stories and insights from the best of the best in the industry, *Mastering Business For Strategic Communicators* must be required reading for students and practitioners alike in any area of business, communication, and public relations.

— *Tina McCorkindale, Ph.D., APR,*
President and Chief Executive Officer,
Institute for Public Relations

An indispensable collection of career-defining insights from an unbelievably impressive group of battle-tested business leaders. This will quickly become mandatory reading for me and my team, and a constant travel companion.

— *Torod Neptune, Worldwide VP Communications and Chief Communications Officer, Lenovo Group, Ltd.*

Backstopping every C-suite are their strategic communications leaders, counseling businesses on how to increase shareholder value, maintain trust in a crisis, and enhance reputation. *Mastering Business* provides a front row seat as to how diverse companies navigate the communications land mines populating our ever changing media landscape.

— *Barri Rafferty, Partner and President, Ketchum*

Mastering Business is a succinct, readable and compelling work. It does a wonderful job capturing the way the profession has evolved and how it might look in the future. The insights here from Jeff Winton, Chuck Greener, Tony Cervone, Kathy Beiser and many other true giants in the field present a blueprint for those who want to be trusted advisors with a seat at the table where business decisions are made. It is an essential read for anyone pursuing a career in communications.

— *Bill Heyman, Executive Recruiter, President and CEO, Heyman Associates*

I've recommended Ragas and Culp's first book, *Business Essentials for Strategic Communicators*, to dozens of professional colleagues and have made it a central textbook for my students.

I can see now that I'll need to make room for their new book, *Mastering Business for Strategic Communicators*. This compilation of perspectives from some of the top names in strategic communications is remarkably timely and thorough, and should be on the top of the reading list not only for communications professionals, but for C-Suite leaders who want to truly understand the role that communications plays in helping them achieve their business purpose.

— Matt Kucharski, President,
Padilla and Adjunct Professor,
University of Minnesota School of Journalism and
Mass Communications

Ragas and Culp's new book provides sound recommendations and actionable steps young communicators can take to make sure they are prepared and able to show maximum value in their roles. Through an excellent collection of relevant stories from some of the world's top communicators, their book is less about earning a seat at the table and more about keeping it throughout your career.

— Matt Tidwell, Ph.D., APR, Program Director,
Master's in Integrated Marketing Communications,
University of Kansas

In a rare collection of contemporary essays from high-ranking professionals in the field, Ragas and Culp offer students an insider's look at how corporate communications experts guide their companies to meet opportunities, manage change, speak the truth and lead. This book — through its research, arguments, testimonials and concrete examples — will be indispensable to readers in accessing the practical business insight necessary for succeeding in today's corporate communications jobs.

— María Len-Ríos, Ph.D., Associate Professor, Public
Relations, Grady College of Journalism and Mass
Communication, University of Georgia

Ragas and Culp provide an extensive follow-up to their first book, *Business Essentials for Strategic Communicators*. This new book delivers what the title promises: sharp insights from today's leading communication professionals in the C-Suite. With a glossary, list of resources, and engaging writing style, the book will be a valuable trove of knowledge and inspiration for students as well as current professionals aspiring to the C-suite.

— Tim Penning, Ph.D., APR,
Professor of Advertising and Public Relations,
School of Communications,
Grand Valley State University

The masterful leaders of business communication have done it again. Ron Culp and Matt Ragas put out the no-nonsense handbook for enterprise communicators — and for those of us teaching new-wave students — on the reality of sustaining stakeholder values. On this base, they're now giving us direct, succinct and highly readable counsel from leaders in corporations and organizations on what works and what's changing in enterprise strategies to sustain and strengthen critical stakeholder connections.

— E. Bruce Harrison, Professor, Graduate Studies,
Master's in Public Relations & Corporate
Communications program, Georgetown University

The modern communications professional not only needs to be familiar with the "business of business," but rather they need to be able to understand what the marketing, finance, accounting and other departments contribute to their organization's wellbeing. Culp and Ragas' *Mastering Business for Strategic Communicators* takes that next step from their previous book by providing real-world advice from legends and experts in the field that already have that seat at the table. Any communications professional who wants to become a top-level executive needs to read this book.

Mastering Business is a great resource for young professionals who aspire to advance to management positions. I especially appreciated the inclusion of views from other members of the C-suite such as operations, human resources, legal and CEOs. The advice the CCOs provided is grounded in their personal experiences, which they freely share. I would highly recommend this book for young professionals, students, and especially courses in management and leadership.

Ragas and Culp have produced an eminently useful guide to the business of strategic communication. We hear first-hand from leading practitioners what it means to be a strategist-advisor to the C-suite, speaking the language of business and adding bottom-line value. *Mastering Business* is our seat at the table — and a glimpse into the future of the discipline.

In *Business Essentials for Strategic Communicators*, Ragas and Culp gave PR students and rising professionals across the country a roadmap to understanding the critical business skills that would put them on the path to getting a "seat at the table" when key decisions are made. With *Mastering Business*, they bring forward the perspectives and life lessons of some of the most respected leaders in corporate communications, giving us not only an engaging read but also a master class in what to do once you have the seat at the table, and more importantly how to keep it. It's a must read for anyone who wants to be a CCO or plans to work with one.

— *Ken Kerrigan, Executive Vice President,*
Weber Shandwick, and Adjunct Professor,
MS in Public Relations and Corporate
Communication program, New York University

Mastering Business clearly spells out the skills inherent in the business acumen of top leaders. If you hold a high-level communications role within an organization or have ever aspired to such a position, you would be well served to spend next weekend reading *Mastering Business*, a thought-provoking and brilliant book.

— *Timothy Lent Howard, Ph.D.,*
Professor of Public Relations,
California State University, Sacramento

Writing and persuasion is no longer enough. In order to be successful, today's communication professionals *need* to have a solid understanding of the world of business. With the essays presented in this book, Ragas and Culp have brought together a venerable "who's who" of communication executives from across industries and business sectors. The keen wisdom and practical insights they share will prove invaluable not only to students of strategic communication but also professionals already in the industry.

— Nathan Gilkerson, Ph.D., Assistant Professor,
Strategic Communication,
Diederich College of Communication,
Marquette University

Who else but seasoned CCOs could transform the complexity of business management into straightforward, engaging stories that synthesize years of corporate communications wisdom? *Mastering Business for Strategic Communicators* is a must read for aspiring communicators looking to break into the corporate world.

— Christopher Wilson, Ph.D.,
Assistant Professor, Public Relations,
School of Communications,
Brigham Young University

MASTERING BUSINESS FOR STRATEGIC COMMUNICATORS

Insights and Advice from the
C-suite of Leading Brands

Edited by

MATTHEW W. RAGAS
DePaul University, USA

RON CULP
DePaul University, USA

United Kingdom — North America — Japan — India — Malaysia — China

Emerald Publishing Limited
Howard House, Wagon Lane, Bingley BD16 1WA, UK

First edition 2018

Copyright © 2018 Emerald Publishing Limited

Reprints and permissions service
Contact: permissions@emeraldinsight.com

British Library Cataloguing in Publication Data
A catalogue record for this book is available from the British Library

ISBN: 978-1-78743-821-7 (Print)
ISBN: 978-1-78714-503-0 (Online)
ISBN: 978-1-78714-952-6 (Epub)

ISOQAR certified
Management System,
awarded to Emerald
for adherence to
Environmental
standard
ISO 14001:2004.

ISOQAR
REGISTERED

Certificate Number 1985
ISO 14001

INVESTOR IN PEOPLE

This book is dedicated to our better halves, Traci and Sandra,
and our students, who inspire us each and every day,
and are the future leaders of our field.

CONTENTS

PART III

FINANCE AND INVESTOR RELATIONS

PART IV

HUMAN RESOURCES AND EMPLOYEE ENGAGEMENT

PART V

CORPORATE STRATEGY, INNOVATION, AND LEGAL

PART IX

SUMMING UP

LIST OF CONTRIBUTORS

Stephen B. Ashley	Fannie Mae, The Ashley Companies
Mark Bain	upper 90 consulting, Baker McKenzie
Kathryn Beiser	Edelman, Hilton Worldwide
Roger Bolton	Arthur W. Page Society
Maureen Cahill	Blue Cross Blue Shield Association
Carole Casto	Cummins Inc.
Tony Cervone	General Motors
Sean Connolly	Conagra Brands
Ron Culp	DePaul University
Corey duBrowa	Salesforce, Starbucks
Paul Edwards	General Motors
Steve Fechheimer	Beam Suntory
Paul Gerrard	Blue Cross Blue Shield Association
Chuck Greener	Walgreens Boots Alliance
Roy Guthrie	Discover Financial Services
Jon Harris	Conagra Brands
Gavin Hattersley	MillerCoors
Lucy Helm	Starbucks
Clarkson Hine	Beam Suntory
Jeff Immelt	General Electric
Joe Jacuzzi	Chevrolet, General Motors
Richard Kylberg	Arrow Electronics
Mike Long	Arrow Electronics
Peter Marino	MillerCoors, Tenth and Blake Beer Company
Bill McDermott	SAP
Kelly McGinnis	Levi Strauss & Co.
Craig Meurlin	Amway Corp.
Tom Nealon	Southwest Airlines
Matt Peacock	Vodafone Group
Matthew W. Ragas	DePaul University

Angela Roberts	American Veterinary Medical Association, Blue Cross Blue Shield Association
Jim Robinson	Astellas Americas
Linda Rutherford	Southwest Airlines
Stacy Sharpe	Allstate Insurance Company
Steve Shebik	Allstate Insurance Company
Gary Sheffer	Weber Shandwick
Andrew Solomon	John D. and Catherine T. MacArthur Foundation
Julia Stasch	John D. and Catherine T. MacArthur Foundation
Rick Stephens	Boeing
Amy Summy	TE Connectivity
B.J. Talley	TE Connectivity
Serpil Timuray	Vodafone Group
Anne C. Toulouse	Boeing
Nick Tzitzon	SAP
Jeffrey A. Winton	Astellas Pharma
Elizabeth Wood	Levi Strauss & Co.

ACKNOWLEDGMENTS

The authors wish to thank the many educators, professionals, students, and colleagues who have encouraged us to write, speak, and teach on business acumen. Your support for our first book together, *Business Essentials for Strategic Communicators*, inspired us to tackle such an ambitious project as this next book *Mastering Business for Strategic Communicators: Insights and Advice from the C-suite of Leading Brands*. We are especially indebted to all of the contributors to this book who took time out of their hectic schedules to share their insights and experiences as Chief Communications Officers (CCO) with the next generation of strategic communications leaders.

We are grateful for the support of our outstanding editor, Charlotte Maiorana, and the talented team at Emerald Group Publishing. Charlotte saw both the value and need for this book from the start. We wish to thank our previous editor-turned-literary agent, Leila Campoli, for her continued guidance and support. A special thank you is owed to Kevin Spitta, our graduate assistant during our editing of this book. Kevin kept a complicated project with many moving parts and deadlines beautifully organized, and always did so with a smile and an encouraging word. We can't wait to follow his career. Thank you also to Dean Salma Ghanem and our colleagues in the College of Communication at DePaul University. You inspire us with your steadfast commitment to investing in students and making the world a better place.

Feedback from the educators, professionals, and students that supported *Business Essentials*, and the counsel they provided during the writing and editing of *Mastering Business* was critical. We especially wish to thank faculty for incorporating business essentials education into their courses at colleges and universities that include: American University, Baylor University, Boston University, Brigham Young University, California State University, Sacramento, Columbia University, Florida Gulf Coast University, Georgetown University, Grand Valley State University, Loyola University (Chicago), Marquette University, New York University, Northwestern University, Medill School, University of Alabama, University of Georgia, University of Minnesota, and University of Southern California, Annenberg School. Apologies for any we may have missed. Senior leaders in both agencies and in-house roles have also used *Business Essentials* with their teams as a training and development tool, and we appreciate and enjoy the opportunities to speak and work with their teams on this capability.

The future of the public relations and strategic communications fields is in good hands in part because of the excellent academic and professional groups in our profession, and the dedicated leaders and volunteers that guide these organizations. We wish to thank the following associations and centers for all they do: Arthur W. Page Society and Page Up, The Arthur W. Page Center for Integrity in Public Communications, Association for Education in Journalism and Mass Communication (AEJMC), Association for Measurement and Evaluation of Communication (AMEC), Business Marketing Association (BMA), Commission on Public Relations Education (CPRE), Corporate Communication International, International Association of Business Communicators (IABC), International Public Relations Research Conference (IPRRC), Institute for Public Relations (IPR), International Communication Association (ICA), The Museum of Public Relations, National Investor Relations Institute (NIRI), The Plank Center for Leadership in Public Relations, the PR Council, PRSA Foundation, Publicity Club of Chicago (PCC), Public Relations Society of

America (PRSA) and Public Relations Student Society of America (PRSSA), and USC Center for Public Relations.

Matthew wishes to thank his parents and family for instilling in him a love of learning at an early age. Whether it was an early interest in history (his mom will tell you he tried to write the history of the world), reading, writing, the news media, politics, or the world of business, all interests were encouraged and supported. He didn't just read or watch business news growing up, but, thanks to his parents, he was able to track a real portfolio of stocks and follow their performance. He was also given nothing but encouragement around his entrepreneurial business ideas and his work in start-up companies — some that succeeded tremendously, while others crashed and burned. Either way, his parents were always there to encourage his latest and greatest. Matthew also wishes to thank the mentors that have enriched his professional and personal development, including Edward P. "Ned" Grace III, Spiro Kiousis, and Ron Culp. Take note future communications leaders: Ron shows that "work hard and be nice" is the right way to lead.

Ron also thanks his DePaul colleagues and other educators who so warmly welcomed him into academia after a long career in corporate and agency roles. As a self-described "pracademic," Ron appreciates the encouragement and support being given to increasing experiential opportunities for both students and those teaching them. To that end, he wishes to salute the Plank Center for Leadership in Public Relations for its role in bridging gaps between educators and professionals. Like Matt, Ron also thanks his mentors and friends, many of whom are no longer with us — the late Betsy Plank, Dan Edelman, Al Golin, and Jack Raymond. They and others have had a huge influence on his life and career. Ron also thanks colleague and friend Matthew Ragas and hundreds of other mentees who have been so instrumental to his life and career. Each and every one has proven that mentorship, indeed, is a two-way street. These future leaders of our profession are doing things each and every day that make him proud.

Finally, thanks to you, the reader. Your interest in business acumen and strategic communication leadership will not only benefit you and your career, but the overall stature of the profession and its ability to create value for both business and society as a whole.

Matthew W. Ragas

Ron Culp

Chicago, IL.

PREFACE

Strategic communication increasingly means business.

Recognition is growing among communication professionals, educators, and organizational leaders that — for communications departments and agencies to provide the most value to organizations, their stakeholders, and society as a whole — strategic communicators need to be *business people with an expertise in communication.*

Let this last sentence sink in for a moment, as it represents a paradigm shift of sorts.

Fortunately, inside many large organizations the communications function increasingly has gained the trust of members of the C-suite on advising these senior leaders on "what to do" — policy setting — and not just "what to say" or "how to say it."

The role of being both counselor and advisor — rather than simply that of a skilled communications technician — demands greater business acumen, not just for the chief communications officer (CCO) or senior agency professionals, but for mid- and junior-level team members who help support these leaders. The entire profession and, in fact, society as a whole benefits when more pros improve their fluency in the language and essentials of business, thereby better shaping and communicating purpose and strategy across an enterprise and outside of it. It is perhaps a misnomer to label the field "strategic communications" if professionals are well versed in technical skills, but lack a strategic business management perspective.

The good news is that we have seen firsthand how agencies, in-house teams, and university communication programs are placing a greater emphasis on building business acumen. The very positive response by professionals and educators to our first book together titled, *Business Essentials for Strategic Communicators: Creating Shared Value for the Organization and Its Stakeholders*, is heartening. Reader feedback on *Business Essentials* placed a particular value on the illustrative quotes in the book drawn from original interviews with senior leaders in the field. Business concepts and terminology — and the value of investing in gaining such knowledge — become much more tangible when they are illustrated with real-world stories.

This book, *Mastering Business for Strategic Communicators: Insights and Advice from the C-suite of Leading Brands* builds upon this feedback and the continued evolution of the profession. Strategic communicators have a unique vantage point across both the enterprise and society as a whole. As such, communications leaders are increasingly being asked by the C-suite to serve as conveners, collaborators, and integrators *across departments and functions*. To fulfill such a mandate, communicators need not just general business acumen, but a rich understanding of the major departments and functions that make up the C-suite, such as marketing, finance, human resources, investor relations, corporate strategy, legal, data science, and technology.

As such, *Mastering Business* brings together many top senior communications leaders in the field who generously share both their insights and experiences learned while working with specific C-suite functions and C-level executives. We have purposely drawn contributors that come from a wide range of backgrounds, industries, and geographies to provide a diversity of thought and experiences. Collectively, these contributors help drive the business strategy and protect the corporate reputations of brands that are worth many billions in market value, employ tens of thousands of people, and produce products and services used by millions of people.

Alongside each contributor essay, you will find a short "Career Spotlight" Q&A with this industry leader. In addition, to provide a valuable "outside/inside" perspective, each essay also includes a "C-suite View" response authored by a C-level executive that is a current or former colleague of the contributor. We think you will find these outsider viewpoints illuminating.

We thank these "Masters of Business" for graciously sharing their insights and experiences, and for helping to advance the body of knowledge. Collaborations between educators and practitioners are still far too rare. We offer this book in the hope that it will inspire future such collaboration.

FOREWORD

Matt Ragas' and Ron Culp's first book together, *Business Essentials for Strategic Communicators*, addressed the fundamental truth that understanding how the business works is the price of entry for success in strategic communication.

Their new book, *Mastering Business for Strategic Communicators: Insights and Advice from the C-suite of Leading Brands*, takes the conversation to a new level. Here, we learn how to work across the enterprise with senior leaders who are subject matter experts. Being able to function as a peer — sometimes leading, sometimes following, always collaborating — requires an ability to think strategically about business challenges and a command of the soft, interpersonal skills that distinguish the best leaders. This book contains the stories of successful senior communicators who have mastered both.

When I led strategic communication at Aetna, the company had a near-death experience. The board brought in a new CEO, Jack Rowe, who was determined to turn the company around with a new strategy, a new operating model, and a transformed culture. I supported his focus on quality health care and his ideas about making the company more responsive to physicians and patients, and more focused on facilitating quality health care outcomes. But Jack was replacing most of the senior team and I was taking nothing for granted.

I was called into Jack's office just a few weeks after his arrival and half-expected that he was going to tell me I was out. Instead, Jack said, "I want you to lead the culture change initiative." I was shocked. It wasn't my expertise and I hadn't a clue how to go about it.

The task was immense. Aetna was a 150-year-old company with an entrenched, risk-averse, process-oriented, insurance company culture. It had recently acquired an entrepreneurial, process-averse company and the merger of the two businesses had led to a bitter culture war.

We had to lose the allegiances to the previous entities and think through objectively what cultural attributes would be needed to support the new strategy and operating model, both of which were simultaneously under development. We asked ourselves, *who owns the culture?* The answer: no single executive or department — not HR and not even the CEO. We *all* had to own it *together*.

I formed a partnership with my close colleague, Elease Wright, who led human resources, and consultant Jon Katzenbach. To lead the work, we created an ad hoc Council for Organizational Effectiveness. By Jack's edict, every line and staff organization in the company had to be represented by a senior executive. It was my job to bring along everyone — even the foot-draggers — by gradually building small successes into bigger ones.

Fortunately, my background working in politics and at IBM had prepared me well for the kind of collaboration this task required. I had learned you need three things:

1. *Have a clue*: You must understand the business. In this case, I had to learn how the culture impacted operations and strategy. You may never be as knowledgeable as the functional experts, but if you can't understand and think strategically about complex topics, you will be marginalized.

2. *Have guts*: All enterprises have a tendency to develop groupthink. We work together, understand each other, and share the same experiences. That's a strength, but when change is

necessary, it takes courage to stand up against the conventional wisdom.

3. *Have woo*: Okay, I know that woo is a verb, but I like Strengthsfinder's definition: "People with the strength of WOO have a great capacity to inspire and motivate others." Building alliances with battle-hardened executives requires the skills that communicators should be really good at: *active listening* and *thoughtful persuasion*.

Our council met monthly, gathering input from across the organization and creating a new mission statement, a set of values and operating principles. Most important, we built commitment to the new culture through both processes and dialogue. Employees were skeptical at first, and there were pockets of resistance. But our enterprise-wide approach developed evangelists throughout the organization who kept us focused and committed. By the time Jack and I left six years later, the company had rebuilt its pride and its financial success.

Matthew and Ron bring the deep knowledge of successful educators and practitioners to this project. They have assembled here a set of essays from some of the world's leading communicators that illustrate how to work effectively with senior business leaders across departments and functions.

This is a timely contribution, because corporate communication is more critical to the success of the enterprise than ever before. Strategic communication leaders must rally support *across the enterprise* to build a corporate character that makes the organization worthy of trust, and simultaneously must enlist the entire enterprise to build authentic stakeholder engagement.

You will want to keep your copy close at hand as an essential resource.

Roger Bolton
President
Arthur W. Page Society

PART I

INTRODUCTION

1

ADVISING "THE ROOM WHERE IT HAPPENS": THE BUSINESS CASE FOR BUSINESS ACUMEN

Matthew W. Ragas and Ron Culp
DePaul University

I wanna be in the room where it happens.

Before this was a line from a hit song in the smash Broadway musical "Hamilton," strategic communications professionals had argued that — for them to do their jobs most effectively — they needed a "seat at the table" or access to this table (Bowen, 2008, 2009; Grunig, Grunig, & Dozier, 2002; Harrison & Mühlberg, 2015; Turk, 1989). Research shows that, over the past decade, the chief communications officer (CCO) increasingly *is* part of an organization's leadership team (Marshall, Fowler, & Olson, 2015a, 2015b; Swerling et al., 2014), or at least advises members of the C-suite (APCO Worldwide, 2016), including sitting on executive-level committees (Neill, 2015). In a more transparent world, in which companies must earn and keep the trust of their stakeholders, and corporate reputations and brands can provide competitive advantage (Doorley & Garcia, 2015; Goodman & Hirsch, 2015), the roles, responsibilities, and expectations of the CCO and strategic communicators have been elevated (Sahel, 2017).

With this elevation of communications within corporations, the knowledge, skills, and capabilities required of not just the CCO, but of the in-house and agency professionals that support the communications function, is transforming. Both professionals and academics alike (e.g., Feldman, 2016; Marron, 2014; Neill & Schauster, 2015; Ragas, Uysal, & Culp, 2015; Roush, 2006) have discussed the evolving skillset required for communication professionals to truly be *strategic assets* to their organizations in advancing corporate character, purpose, goals, objectives, and strategies (Berger & Meng, 2014; Dolphin & Fan, 2000; Laskin, 2011).

KNOWLEDGE, SKILLS, AND CAPABILITIES FOR FUTURE LEADERS

Generally, professionals and educators agree (Duhé, 2013; Feldman, 2016; Kolberg, 2014; PRNews Pro, 2016a, 2016b; Spangler, 2014) that a strong grounding in the fundamentals of the major areas of business, such as management, finance, accounting, marketing, sales, human resources, information technology and data science, supply chain, innovation and transformation, is an important knowledge base for communicators (Claussen, 2008; DiStaso, Stacks, & Botan, 2009; Ragas, 2016; Wright, 1995, 2011). This essential general and industry-specific business knowledge is often referred to by professionals as *business acumen* (Charan, 2001; Cope, 2012; Ragas & Culp, 2013, 2014a, 2014b, 2015). While learning about *the business of business* has long been espoused by some educators as critical to training future strategic communications professionals (e.g., Turk, 1989; Wright, 1995), this perspective has gained broader acceptance in recent years (see Commission on Public Relations Education, 2012, 2015).

For example, Dennis Wilcox and Glen Cameron outline six essential career skills in *Public Relations: Strategies and Tactics* (2012), one of the most widely used textbooks in public relations classrooms. These skills are: (1) effective writing, (2) research ability, (3) planning expertise, (4) problem-solving ability, (5) business/economics competence, and (6) expertise in social media. Wilcox and Cameron (2012) write that "the increasing emphasis on public relations as a management function calls for public relations students to learn the 'nuts and bolts' of business and economics" (p. 25). An important argument can be made that professionals sharpen some of these essential skills, such as problem-solving ability, through having a stronger and deeper understanding of business, thereby better understanding possible solutions to problems.

Of course, it is important to emphasize that business acumen is not a "be all, end all" in itself for strategic communication success or the advancement of the profession. Some studies show a greater importance (Neill & Schauster, 2015; Ragas et al., 2015) placed on business acumen by practitioners than others (Sievert, Rademacher, & Weber, 2016). For example, the 2017 *Global Communication Report* from the USC Center for Public Relations found that, when given a list of important skills for future growth, professionals rated business literacy (64% rated as important) in the middle of the pack with strategic planning (89%) at the top and media buying (18%) at the bottom. Of course, to gain a "big picture" view so as to make meaningful contributions to strategic planning, a professional needs a strong grounding in general business acumen, as well as the specifics of an industry and organization.

THE NEW CCO

The Arthur W. Page Society, a professional association comprised of senior strategic communications professionals, agency heads, and distinguished academics from around the world, has done perhaps the most detailed multi-year research and thought leadership work examining the future knowledge, skills, and capabilities required of CCOs and professionals working in corporate communication. This mixed-methods research program conducted by the Arthur W. Page Society (2016, 2017a) concludes that the CCO and communications function of tomorrow will serve the following roles in activating corporate character (Arthur W. Page Society, 2013a, 2013b) and building authentic advocacy (Arthur W. Page Society, 2007):

(1) *The foundational CCO*: The CCO will be expected to serve as a strategic business leader and counselor, a steward of enterprise reputation and an effective communicator.

(2) *The CCO as integrator*: The CCO will be expected to drive cross-functional collaboration and integration on strategic priorities across the enterprise. As such, the CEO should have a direct working relationship with the CEO and C-suite colleagues.

(3) *The CCO as builder of digital engagement systems*: The CCO will be expected to leverage data to understand individuals; create channels and platforms to connect with those individuals directly; and engage with individuals to shape opinion and influence behavior.

In assessing the changing organizational landscape, Bob Feldman, co-founder and principal of PulsePoint Group and co-chair of the Arthur W. Page Society's skills and capabilities committee, has argued that "basic business skills are still required" and "the need for general leadership skills is stronger than ever" (Feldman, 2016, para. 1). Based on feedback from Page Society members and members of Page Up, a sister organization, the following capabilities were identified as being the most critical for professionals:

- Strategic business thinking

- Dealing with ambiguity and complexity

- Offering courageous counsel

- Problem solving

- Business acumen

Feldman sees the lack of greater levels of business acumen across the PR and corporate communication fields as inhibiting how the function is perceived by business leaders:

> *The rise of the entire function in the eyes of the C-suite depends on the stature, business acumen and performance of the individuals in the organization. Strong business acumen is not perceived to exist now in the function, meaning it will often be viewed as a tactical, non-strategic weapon. (2016, para. 9)*

These remarks generally align with the discussions among Page Society and Page Up members during a multi-day, global online brainstorm, called a Page Jam, held in fall 2014 about the future of the CCO and corporate communications. John Onoda, a senior consultant at FleishmanHillard and previously a senior communications executive for brands such as Charles Schwab, General Motors, Visa USA, and Levi Strauss, offered the following perspective based on his decades of leadership experience: "When I think about my relationship with the different CEOs and chairmen I've worked with, it was probably my business acumen more than my communication skills that most strengthened the bond between us."

On a related note, in this same Page Jam, James S. O'Rourke, professor of management and former director of the Fanning Center for Business Communication at the University of Notre Dame, argued that having business acumen simply makes for better informed and more effective strategic communications

professionals. According to O'Rourke, "Unless we each understand how our companies make money, how they grow or gain
market share, and how they compete directly in the marketspace,
our story-telling is likely to come off as superficial or shallow."

Arthur W. Page Society (2017a) research has also interviewed
more than 20 CEOs of large corporations to gain their opinions
on the roles and expectations they have today of CCOs and the
communications function as a whole. This research concludes that
total business knowledge by the CCO is now "table stakes."
More specifically, this CEO research finds that:

> *In years past, CEOs have expressed* hope *that their CCO
> would know all about their enterprise's business in order
> to more strategically apply communications to advance
> its goals. Now, many CEOs* require *their CCO to be
> knowledgeable about the business — from strategy to
> operations — so they are able to provide strategic input
> on issues that span business functions.*

Such a statement indicates that the communications staff and
external partners supporting CCOs will be better positioned to do
so by sharpening their business knowledge and skills.

THE CCO'S EXPANDING LEADERSHIP ROLE

Complementing the Page Society research on the new CCO and the
future of the communications function, the Korn Ferry Institute, the
research and analytics arm of Korn Ferry, the world's largest executive search, leadership and talent development firm, has also has
conducted research with CCOs on this subject (Marshall et al.
2015a, 2015b). As with the Page Society, the Korn Ferry research
finds that CCOs of FORTUNE 500 companies believe they are
generally taking on a more prominent leadership role within their
organizations. Further, they feel that having a "strategic mind-set"

is their most important leadership characteristic. More specifically, according to the survey results, "The CCO, as with other C-suite roles, is expected to contribute in shaping enterprise strategy" (Marshall et al., 2015a, p. 2).

Continuing with this theme, the Korn Ferry Institute research recommends:

> *The more adept Fortune 500 CCOs become in strategic roles — even to the point of becoming elite corporate affairs strategist-advisors — the more they will be recognized not only for their expertise in developing integrated and aligned communications strategies but also for their ability to help develop organizational strategies involving a wide variety of constituents and stakeholders. (Marshall et al., 2015a, p. 3)*

The survey results (Marshall et al., 2015a, p. 5) indicate that — beyond managing the traditional communications function — CCOs and their teams are being asked to demonstrate leadership on:

- Reputation, values, and culture across the enterprise
- Design systems, such as those that support an enterprise-wide social media strategy
- Define and activate corporate character
- Develop and publish content for external stakeholders
- Analyze data to understand how stakeholders view the enterprise

The study authors (Marshall et al., 2015a) recommend that CCOs gain broader experiences and develop deeper financial and business acumen so as to be better prepared to assume broader leadership responsibilities. A separate study by the Korn Ferry Institute (Marshall et al., 2015b) identifies an elite sub-set of CCOs that it calls a "best-in-class corporate affairs executive"

(p. 1), whom serves as an advisor-strategist to the CEO and the C-suite, counseling through the lens of anything that may impact the corporation's brand and reputation.

ADVISING THOSE "IN THE ROOM WHERE IT HAPPENS"

"You cannot *not* communicate" is the new reality for corporations in a hyper-connected world in which every move, whether made by management or front-line employees, is monitored and evaluated by stakeholders — and can bolster or sink brands and reputations in a flash.

As such, CCOs and communication departments are increasingly being called upon to define, activate and align company values, corporate character, and culture across the enterprise — from the board room to the front lines. Further, a growing number of CCOs and their departments are being asked to provide strategic counsel so that corporate behaviors *hold true* to such values, character, and culture. Companies deserving of trust don't simply "talk the talk," but they "walk the walk." CCOs and senior communications professionals need direct access to the CEO and the C-suite so as to have meaningful input into both decision-making and the development of corporate strategy, rather than simply being brought in *after the fact* to communicate such decisions and policies within the enterprise and to external stakeholders.

Decades of business management research around signaling theory (Spence, 1973, 2002) and reducing information asymmetry (Stiglitz, 2002a, 2002b) demonstrates that often the most powerful "signals" that companies send to stakeholders and markets are through the *actions* they take, rather than simply the *words* they say, whether that be through news releases or social media messages. There is an old adage on Wall Street that implores investors to "watch what they do and not what they say" when it comes to monitoring and evaluating the senior leadership of corporations. Whenever a company takes an observable action such as changing an HR policy, adopting a new CSR initiative or the handling of a crisis, it communicates, or sends a signal, to stakeholders and the general public about the underlying qualities of the organization, including its character, reputation, and culture (Connelly, Certo, Ireland, & Reutzel, 2011).

The writings and speeches of pioneering corporate communications executive Arthur W. Page is the inspiration for the organization's Page Principles. The second Page principle, only after "tell the truth," is "prove it with action" (Arthur W. Page Society, 2017b, para. 3). According to this principle, "public perception of an enterprise is determined 90 percent by what it does and 10 percent by what it says" (Arthur W. Page Society, 2017b, para. 3). While the exact ratio is debatable, the general advice is hard to debate and it is backed by empirical research (see the voluminous literature on signaling theory and related perspectives): *actions often speak louder than words.*

A real-world case example is illustrative. In April 2017, United Airlines faced a global firestorm following the decision to involuntarily remove an already seated passenger, Dr. David Dao, from one of its planes, due to an overbooking situation (Mutzabaugh, 2017; Tangel & Carey, 2017). Passenger videos of Dr. Dao being forcefully dragged off the flight went viral via social media and cable news. There was speculation that the initial widely criticized statements issued by United in the aftermath might have been different if the company's CCO had reported directly to the CEO rather than United's head of human resources (McGregor, 2017). Perhaps more important than reporting relationships is that the CCO is a trusted and valued source of advice to the C-suite, and has direct access to the CEO during such events (Neill, 2015).

What is not debatable is that, in the weeks following the crisis, United CEO Oscar Munoz sent a letter to all customers titled, "Actions Speak Louder than Words" (United Airlines Inc., 2017).

In the letter, Munoz blamed the situation on corporate policies that were "placed ahead of our shared values" and said the airline could "never say we are sorry enough for what occurred, but we also know meaningful actions will speak louder than words" (United Airlines Inc., 2017, para. 4). More specifically, in response to the crisis, United announced 10 new or updated customer service policies as part of its "Review and Action Report" and reached a settlement with the injured passenger (Mutzabaugh, 2017; Tangel & Carey, 2017). Once again, *prove it with action.*

CHALLENGES AND OPPORTUNITIES FOR THE CCO

There is perhaps a fixation at times on the CCO officially becoming a member of the C-suite and having the proverbial "seat at the table." Public relations scholar Marlene Neill (2015) calls this "an example of tunnel vision" (p. 130). Many successful CCOs and senior strategic communications executives operate within organizational structures that do not have direct reporting lines to the CEO. The future of the CCO and strategic communications as a whole relies on earning (and keeping) a role as a trusted advisor to the C-suite so that corporate actions and words are better aligned behind strategies that create both financial and social value (Bowen, 2008, 2009). This can happen with the CCO officially a member of the C-suite or the CCO advising the C-suite and CEO from outside of the room. What is most critical is that *it happens.*

Business is being transformed and, with it, the structure, functioning, and integration of departments (Haran & Sheffer, 2015; USC Annenberg Center for Public Relations, 2017), and the perceived value they provide to the enterprise. With the growing integration of communications and marketing, and an increased focus on data analytics to measure, demonstrate and improve business results, the Chief Marketing Officer's (CMO) influence is also on the rise and their scope is broadening (Daniels, 2015). A possible outcome of such integration is that public relations could become more of a sub-set of marketing (USC Annenberg Center for Public Relations, 2017). On a related note, in a world in which every company is becoming a technology company, the influence and scope of the Chief Technology Officer (CTO) and Chief Information Officer (CIO) is also growing within many organizations.

There is no doubt that the CCO and strategic communicators bring unique perspectives and value to the table for the C-suite. A well-established communications function offers forward-looking 360 degree views and insights into *all* of an enterprise's stakeholders, from employees and suppliers to policymakers and other opinion leaders. Such perspective is unique and important in protecting and growing brands and reputations in a stakeholder-empowered world. But every corporate function feels it is valuable and worthy of counseling the C-suite and sitting on executive-level committees. Without improving and expanding the skills and capabilities of its future leaders, strategic communications and public relations could be at a risk of being diminished in this changing business landscape (Groysberg, 2014).

Business acumen is not a magic elixir for the profession, but it certainly must be an important factor. If communicators are serious about approaching their jobs as *business people with an expertise in communications*, then the entire field — from educators and students to mid-career professionals right up to senior leaders — needs to re-double its focus and investment in sharpening its business skills. To be a valued partner to the C-suite and senior leaders means offering sound strategic thinking and communications execution around business problems.

The more than twenty very accomplished CCO contributors found in the following pages are ready and willing to be your professors. So are their C-level colleagues. *Class starts now.*

REFERENCES

APCO Worldwide (2016, November). *Chief corporate communicator survey.* Chicago, IL: APCOWorldwide.

Arthur W. Page Society. (2007). *The authentic enterprise: An Arthur W. Page Society report.* New York, NY: Arthur W. Page Society.

Arthur W. Page Society. (2013a). *Corporate character: How leading companies are defining, activating and aligning values.* New York, NY: Arthur W. Page Society.

Arthur W. Page Society. (2013b). *The CEO view: The impact of communications on corporate character in a 24×7 digital world.* New York, NY: Arthur W. Page Society.

Arthur W. Page Society. (2016). *The new CCO: Transforming enterprises in a changing world.* New York, NY: Arthur W. Page Society.

Arthur W. Page Society. (2017a). *The CEO view: Communications at the center of the enterprise.* Retrieved from http://bit.ly/2q4t2UI. Accessed on May 4, 2017.

Arthur W. Page Society. (2017b). The Page principles. *AWPageSociety.com.* Retrieved from http://www.awpagesociety. com/site/the-page-principles. Accessed on May 1, 2017.

Berger, B. K., & Meng, J. (Eds.). (2014). *Public relations leaders as sensemakers: A global study of leadership in public relations and communication management.* New York, NY: Routledge.

Bowen, S. A. (2008). A state of neglect: Public relations as "corporate conscience" or ethics counsel. *Journal of Public Relations Research, 20*(3), 271–296.

Bowen, S. A. (2009). What communication professionals tell us regarding dominant coalition access and gaining membership.

Journal of Applied Communication Research, 37(4), 418–443. doi:1080/00909880903233184

Charan, R. (2001). *What the CEO wants you to know: Using business acumen to understand how your company really works.* New York, NY: Crown Business.

Claussen, D. (2008). On the business and economics education of public relation students. *Journalism & Mass Communication Educator*, 63(3), 191–194.

Commission on Public Relations Education. (2012, October). *Standards for a master's degree in public relations: Educating for complexity.* New York, NY: The Commission on Public Relations Education.

Commission on Public Relations Education. (2015, May). *Summary report: Commission on Public Relations Education's (CPRE) industry-educator summit on public relations education.* New York, NY: The Commission on Public Relations Education.

Connelly, B. L., Certo, S. T., Ireland, R. D., & Reutzel, C. R. (2011). Signaling theory: A review and assessment. *Journal of Management*, 37(1), 39–67. doi:10.1177/0149206310388419

Cope, K. (2012). *Seeing the big picture: Business acumen to build your credibility, career and company.* Austin, TX: Greenleaf Book Group Press.

Daniels, C. (2015, April 10). How the CCO role is changing – It's complicated. *PR Week*. Retrieved from http://bit.ly/1yjqReE. Accessed on May 1, 2017.

DiStaso, M. W., Stacks, D. W., & Botan, C. H. (2009). State of public relations education in the United States: 2006 report on a national survey of executives and academics. *Public Relations Review*, 35(3), 254–269. doi:10.1016/j. pubrev.2009.03.006

Dolphin, R. R., & Fan, D. (2000). Is corporate communications a strategic function? *Management Decision, 38*(2), 99–106.

Doorley, J., & Garcia, H. F. (2015). *Reputation management: The key to successful public relations and corporate communication* (3rd ed.). New York, NY: Routledge.

Duhé, S. (2013, December 12). *Teaching business as a second language*. Institute for Public Relations. Retrieved from http://bit.ly/1cGKcsw. Accessed on April 21, 2017.

Feldman, B. (2016, November 28). Dear comms exec: Basic business skills are still required. *PRWeek*. Retrieved from http://bit.ly/2ovUmWt. Accessed on April 20, 2017.

Goodman, M. B., & Hirsch, P. B. (2015). *Corporate communication: Critical business asset for strategic global change*. New York, NY: Peter Lang.

Groysberg, B. (2014, March 18). The seven skills you need to thrive in the C-suite. *Harvard Business Review*. Retrieved from http://bit.ly/2cuwDFX. Accessed on May 8, 2017.

Grunig, L. A., Grunig, J. E., & Dozier, D. M. (2002). *Excellent public relations and effective organizations: A study of communication management in three countries*. Mahwah, NJ: Erlbaum.

Haran, L., & Sheffer, G. (2015, March 24). Is the chief communications officer position going the way of the dodo? *PRWeek*. Retrieved from http://bit.ly/1OLpY3z. Accessed on May 1, 2017.

Harrison, E. B., & Mühlberg, J. (2015). *Leadership communication: How leaders communicate and how communicators lead in today's global enterprise*. New York, NY: Business Expert Press.

Kolberg, B. (2014, March). Getting down to business at public relations agencies. *PR Update, 49*(2), 6–7.

Laskin, A. V. (2011). How investor relations contributes to the corporate bottom line. *Journal of Public Relations Research*, 23(3), 302–324. doi:10.1080/1062726X.2011.582206

Marron, M. B. (2014). Graduate degrees in journalism and the MBA. *Journalism & Mass Communication Educator*, 69(3), 3–4. doi:10.1177/1077695814523933

Marshall, R., Fowler, B., & Olson, N. (2015a). *The chief communications officer: Survey and finding among the Fortune 500.* Los Angeles, CA: Korn Ferry Institute.

Marshall, R., Fowler, B., & Olson, N. (2015b). *Trusted counsel: CEOs expand C-suite mandate for best-in-class corporate affairs officers.* Los Angeles, CA: Korn Ferry Institute.

McGregor, J. (2017, April 27). The most important United Airlines policy change after its dragging fiasco could also be the hardest. *The Washington Post.* Retrieved from http://wapo.st/2oNsl1V. Accessed on April 30, 2017.

Mutzabaugh, B. (2017, April 27). United Airlines is making these 10 customer-service policy changes. *USA Today.* Retrieved from http://usat.ly/2oMarrd. Accessed on April 30, 2017.

Neill, M. S. (2015). Beyond the C-suite: Corporate communications' power and influence. *Journal of Communication Management*, 19(2), 118–132. doi:10.1108/JCOM-06-2013-0046

Neill, M. S., & Schauster, E. (2015). Gaps in advertising and public relations education: Perspectives of agency leaders. *Journal of Advertising Education*, 19(2), 5–17.

PRNews Pro. (2016a, August 29). PR pros still see writing as key to success, but analytics, digital, business skills also important. *PRNewsPro*, 7, 1, 3, 6.

PRNews Pro. (2016b, September 12). Report card from the academics: Next wave of PR pros lacks sharp writing, presentation skills. *PRNewsPro*, 7, 1, 3, 6.

Ragas, M. (2016). Public relations means business: Addressing the need for greater business acumen. *Journal of Integrated Marketing Communications*, 17, 34.

Ragas, M., & Culp, R. (2013, Spring). Taking care of business: How PR pros and academics can build a stronger profession. *The Public Relations Strategist*, 15–16.

Ragas, M. W., & Culp, R. (2014a). *Business essentials for strategic communicators: Creating shared value for the organization and its stakeholders*. New York, NY: Palgrave Macmillan.

Ragas, M., & Culp, R. (2014b, December, 22). *Public relations and business acumen: Closing the gap*. Institute for Public Relations. Retrieved, from http://bit.ly/16MJ33P. Accessed on May 1, 2017.

Ragas, M., & Culp, R. (2015, May 1). Business weak: Five ways to build greater business acumen. *Public Relations Tactics*, p. 17.

Ragas, M. W., Uysal, N., & Culp, R. (2015). "Business 101" in public relations education: An exploratory survey of senior communication executives. *Public Relations Review*, 41(3), 378–380. doi:10.1016/j.pubrev.2015.02.007

Roush, C. (2006). The need for more business education in mass communication schools. *Journalism & Mass Communication Educator*, 61(2), 195–204.

Sahel, J. (2017, February 14). The inner circle. *Briefings* (Korn Ferry Institute). Retrieved from http://www.kornferry.com/institute/the-inner-circle. Accessed on April 20, 2017.

Sievert, H., Rademacher, L., & Weber, A. (2016). Business knowledge as a limited success factor for communications managers:

Results of a survey in the German-speaking context. In P. S. Bronn & A. Zerfass (Eds.), *The management game of communication* (pp. 3–22). Bingley, UK: Emerald Group Publishing Limited.

Spangler, J. (2014, June 2). Valued communicators understand the business. *Institute for Public Relations*. Retrieved from http:// bit.ly/1xiYB8n. Accessed on June 6, 2014.

Spence, M. (1973). Job market signaling. *Quarterly Journal of Economics, 87*(3), 355–374. doi:10.2307/1882010

Spence, M. (2002). Signaling in retrospect and the informational structure of markets. *American Economic Review, 92,* 434–459.

Stiglitz, J. E. (2002a). Information and the change in the paradigm in economics. *American Economic Review, 92*(3), 460–501. doi:10.1257/00028280260136363

Stiglitz, J. E. (2002b). The contributions of the economics of information to twentieth century economics. *Quarterly Journal of Economics, 115*(4), 1441–1478. doi:10.1162/003355300555015

Swerling, J., Thorson, K., Tenderich, B., Yang, A., Li, Z., Gee, E., & Savastano, E. (2014). *GAP VIII: Eighth communication and public relations generally accepted practices study.* Los Angeles, CA: Strategic Communication & Public Relations Center, Annenberg School for Communication and Journalism, University of Southern California.

Tangel, A., & Carey, S. (2017). United Airlines reaches settlement with passenger dragged off Chicago flight. *The Wall Street Journal*, April 27. Retrieved from http://on.wsj.com/2py9abi. Accessed on April 30, 2017.

Turk, J. V. (1989). Management skills need to be taught in public relations. *Public Relations Review, 15*(1), 38–52.

United Airlines, Inc. (2017, April 27). Actions speak louder than words. *News.United.com*. Retrieved from http://bit.ly/2pM6MxZ. Accessed on May 4, 2017.

USC Annenberg Center for Public Relations. (2017, March). *2017 global communications report*. Los Angeles, CA: USC Annenberg School for Communication and Journalism.

Wilcox, D. L., & Cameron, G. T. (2012). *Public relations: Strategies and tactics* (10th ed.). Boston, MA: Allyn & Bacon.

Wright, D. K. (1995). The role of corporate public relations executives in the future of employee communications. *Public Relations Review*, 21(3), 181–198. doi:10.1016/0363-8111(95)90020-9

Wright, D. K. (2011). History and development of public relations education in North America: A critical analysis. *Journal of Communication Management*, 15(3), 236–255. doi:10.1108/13632541111151005

PART II

COMMUNICATIONS, BUSINESS ACUMEN, AND THE C-SUITE

2

THE COMMUNICATOR AS INTEGRATOR

Gary Sheffer
Weber Shandwick

During a January 2014 blast of arctic wind and snow in eastern
Wisconsin, I learned of a possible acquisition by my company,
General Electric (GE), of one the most important companies
in France. At the time, I was in Waukesha for a visit to a GE
manufacturing plant by President Obama.

A few days earlier, GE Chairman and CEO Jeff Immelt had said
to me, "Why don't you go out there and make sure we do it right,"
meaning the president's visit to the 100-year-old manufacturing
plant. I immediately flew to Waukesha, where I landed in minus
30-degree-wind-chill weather.

Despite the weather and short notice for the visit, the GE team
had things well in hand when I arrived. They had "process
mapped" everything that needed to be done — from putting
a fresh coat of paint on the walls along the president's walking
route to writing remarks for executives to briefing employees who
would met the president.

During one of the "walk through" sessions for the event, GE
Power's lead communicator, Jim Healy, said to me, "I think we
are serious about buying Alstom."

My heart rate jumped and my mind transitioned immediately from one necessary skill for communicators — knowing GE's story and how to use a big platform to tell it — to learning how our Power business makes money and why acquiring Alstom Power & Grid would make it better.

This was going to be a *big deal*, but not in the way I first envisioned it. Alstom made power generation equipment it sold and serviced around the word. It was as important to France in a nationalistic sense as General Motors is to America. More importantly, it was a terrific acquisition for GE — it would bolster the capabilities of GE's energy generation business globally, and it would accelerate GE's strategy to get more revenue from industrial (vs. financial) businesses, which the company's investors were seeking.

In the ensuing two months, I worked with my GE colleagues to prepare for the announcement of the $17 billion acquisition, which, at the time, was the largest in GE's 130-year-history.[1] My main partners in the C-suite were:

- *Investor relations*, which "sold" the deal to investors. They helped me understand the strategic reason for the deal, the price GE was paying, the nitty gritty terms such as breakup fees if the deal failed; and, the deal's impact on GE's earnings estimates. Then I had to translate this information from "investor speak" to plain language for other audiences — employees, regulators, the media, politicians, and customers.

- *The GE Power business*, which had to dig deep to get information on the products and services of both companies and prepare answers for highly complex issues. For example, GE Power mainly made gas-fired turbines, while Alstom made steam turbines. Therefore, the businesses were "complementary," meaning there was little product overlap, which is important to regulators who would review the transaction. Jim and his GE Power communications team also took the lead on employee and customer communications, and cultural integration.

- *The General Counsel and Global Affairs team*, which focused
  on the needed governmental approvals (more than 40!), legislative and regulatory questions, such as what the deal would do
  to global markets for energy products. As a communicator, you
  must understand how regulators in Brussels, Washington,
  Beijing, and elsewhere would view the acquisition and work
  with colleagues to make those approvals happen.

My role was to synthesize this information into a compelling
and persuasive communications plan for all audiences. We did
that with our most important partner in the C-suite, Jeff Immelt.

The deal was his — he had been involved directly in the nego-
tiations and it was important to achieving his goals for GE.
It seemed more "personal" for Jeff than the dozens of other transactions GE had done over his first 12 years as CEO. It came at
a critical time as the company was putting the global financial
crisis behind it and returning to its roots as an industrial power-
house. I not only had to understand the deal, but I had to understand Jeff and his plans for GE.

I spent time with him listening to his vision for the deal,
and factored that in to the communications documents, sometimes overriding investor or legal language. The rest of the team
went ahead to Paris to prep for the announcement; I stayed
behind so I could fly with Jeff and do more preparation on the
plane.

The homework I had done with my GE colleagues, looking
into every corner of the proposed deal, would now put to the
test. On the flight, we would refine messages and documents,
practice Q&A, and prepare for the unexpected, which, of course,
happened.

Someone leaked the story to *Bloomberg* just as we were preparing to depart for Paris to inform the French government and then
to hold a press conference. Caught unaware, the French

C-suite View

By Jeff Immelt, Former Chairman and CEO, General Electric

Good communicators must be good leaders, particularly when a company is facing a reputation challenge or is announcing news that affects employees, share owners, and the public. Being a leader means making sure the communications team has the skills, resources, and judgment to quickly and effectively tell your side of the story. At GE, we call it "Our Story, Our Way."

But that's not all it takes to be a good communications leader.

It also means that you must operate effectively inside the C-suite, learning from and negotiating with other senior executives so that the story is accurate and compelling. This requires providing feedback on whether the company's actions are consistent with your values, providing internal and external context that may affect the action, and keeping an eye out for "what's next" so that you can adjust to changing realities. This takes self-confidence, an open and analytical mind, and most of all, a deep understanding of the company's business goals and strategies.

GE's acquisition of Alstom took many twists and turns. GE's communications team was in the "war room" every day with their colleagues helping to build understanding, trust, and support from employees, investors, and regulators. We had our ups and downs in the process but, ultimately, telling *our story our way* helped win the deal.

At the time of this writing, Jeff Immelt was the chairman and CEO of General Electric. He has since retired after 16 years of leading a transformation of the industrial giant.

government responded angrily and over the next few months would become GE's biggest adversary to the deal.

The French president at first refused to meet with Jeff. I advised Jeff to leave Paris and go back to the United States — "he can't embarrass you like this," I said. Later, I advised Jeff not to speak at a public hearing of French legislators reviewing the deal. In both cases, I was wrong. Jeff rightfully took the long-term view of the importance of the deal and put his personal situation aside.

Soon, competitors jumped in to try and steal the deal from GE. "The deal is good for France, for Alstom and for GE" became our public mantra. This competition for Alstom wasn't just news in France, it was "the news" and we routinely saw ourselves on television entering and leaving meetings.

The GE communications and advertising team held daily "war room" calls and ran a sterling 360-degree internal and external campaign. Jeff promised jobs for France, the most important currency in an economically challenged country. In June, GE finally won the deal and I was proud when a Parisian taxi driver, knowing I worked for GE, said to me, "I am glad you won, GE is good for France." Nothing like having your messaging repeated back to you by a man on the street.

- Here are a few lessons I learned from this transaction:
  - *The communicator must be an integrator*. No one else in the C-suite has as broad a view as the communicator, save the CEO. Being an integrator means ensuring the messaging and documents consider many points of view, but it also means the communicator must push to ensure everyone on the deal team is informed about new developments and differing points of view.

  - *Know all your audiences*. I had failed in one area of preparation: understanding what Alstom meant to France. I had focused too much on investor messaging and not enough on understanding the economic and social climate in France.

○ *Communications is local.* In a world of rising nationalism and populism, local environment awareness is increasingly important.

Career Spotlight

By Gary Sheffer, Senior Corporate Strategist, Weber Shandwick

What was your first job in communications?

At Siena College I had a work study program working in the sports information office. I got the job because of the essay I wrote as part of the admissions process. In it, I talked about my love of writing and sports, and the importance of journalism in the post-Watergate area. I guess it caught someone's eye.

What is a favorite career memory?

My best memories are always about people — the young people who you see grow, or a leader who helps you along the way. If I had to pick one, it was the GE leadership team I worked with during the global financial crisis. It may sound silly to say a crisis was a favorite memory, but we worked closely together — we despaired, we laughed, we worked our asses off. They are all terrific people and I learned so much from them.

What is your career advice?

Own your career. Don't wait around for things to happen, meaning thinking that someone else — your boss — is planning your career for you. Think about your strengths and weaknesses. Seek training, advice, and experience that can address them. Put your hand up for "stretch" assignments. Ask to go to conferences and other training. Own it!

○ *Relentlessly drive your message.* When we landed on a message that worked — GE is good for France — we pounded it through every channel.

○ *Be nimble.* GE pivoted from investors to the French government and then to E.U. regulators in Brussels.

It would take 18 months from start to finish to close the deal. My team had contributed to its success but we also learned many things along the way.

NOTE

1. Figure taken from http://www.genewsroom.com/press-releases/ge-completes-acquisition-alstom-power-and-grid-businesses-282159

3

WHY BUSINESS ACUMEN MATTERS MORE THAN EVER

Peter Marino[a,b]

[a]MillerCoors
[b]Tenth and Blake Beer Company

First, a confession: I majored in Journalism at the University of Wisconsin-Madison, in part, due to my fear of math. The Journalism major and Communications field didn't have any math or quantitative-based requirements. Truthfully, math scared me and Journalism was a math-free sanctuary. However, as I progressed in my career, I realized that my fear was going to defeat me and prevent me from being the best counselor and advisor I could be, not to mention limit my ability to climb the corporate ladder. Why do I bring up my fear of math? Because you will not understand how businesses work and make money without a good grasp of math. You can't understand accounting or economics without math.

C-suite View
By Gavin Hattersley, CEO, MillerCoors

As Pete writes, I need everyone on my team to have a deep knowledge of our business, despite their functional area. As MillerCoors works to get to growth and keep our brands relevant, it's imperative that our team works together to maximize the impact we can make on our business. Whether you are a lawyer, an HR, finance, operations, or communications executive, I expect that my team has a full understanding of their functional areas and our business overall. Running a multi-billion dollar company with the complexity of ours isn't easy and I need my senior leadership team focused on driving our total business forward every day.

For example, if Pete is overseeing Government Relations and is working on a state tax proposal for us, it is very helpful for him to understand our total business in that given state. We may have an operations center in that state or we may source materials for packaging or brewing that would be very helpful to underscore our full business in that state and go a long way in helping us increase our chance of success. Only through an ongoing dialogue with our head of operations and our head of sales would we be able to shed the full light on that topic.

Any young communications professional should act as an *internal news reporter* to understand in-depth each function at the company.

THE "AH-HA" MOMENT: GETTING GRILLED BY MBAS

After several years on the agency side, I decided to venture to a client-side job to round out my experience, choosing to join Miller Brewing Company in 1998. While there, I was expected to help secure earned media for brands like Miller Lite, by creating great PR programs with our agency partner and to sell them into our marketing team. Our marketers were all MBAs and would grill me on the link to the brand positioning, the expected quantifiable impact, the return on investment (ROI), and so on. Those were the easy questions, but I knew I needed more education when I had to understand what an ROI was, let alone how to calculate it. The questions got more complicated from there when these colleagues started discussing tools like conjoint analysis that I felt ill-equipped to answer with anything other than confusion. It was at that moment that I quickly realized I needed to get smarter and an MBA was in my future.

IF YOU CAN'T BEAT'EM, JOIN'EM: TIME TO GET AN MBA

After six years as a PR professional, I decided to look that fear directly in the face and get my MBA at the University of California — Los Angeles (UCLA).

But first, I needed to pass a college Calculus class, my first math class since high school! Lord, help me.

I passed. I enrolled at UCLA as a full-time MBA student and my first semester brought on statistics, accounting, and economics. Talk about baptism by fire. While the first few weeks felt like I was learning a foreign language in a new country, I started to get the hang of it, thanks to great professors and patient students. As my MBA education progressed, my acumen improved and my ability to solve problems with both hard and soft skills came into clearer focus.

PUTTING MY EDUCATION TO WORK

Fast forward to my current role as Chief Public Affairs and Communications; I am far more effective in my role given my knowledge of economics, accounting, and finance. As a member of our senior leadership team, I sit on a variety of committees that direct the future of our business. I am a member of the operating committee where we debate and discuss large scale capital requests on behalf of the company, from approving a multi-million dollar aluminum pint line in one of our breweries or an alliance partnership with a professional sports franchise like the Atlanta Braves, or just about anything in between. And, I sit on the strategy committee where we discuss possible acquisitions, new product development, and other significant strategic initiatives.

Understanding the business case, the return on capital and how each of these initiatives will impact our business is critical. Functionally, my boss (the CEO) demands that I advise the company on all matters relating to government affairs, community affairs, environmental sustainability, alcohol responsibility, and communications. That's a big part of my job and requires a deep understanding of our business. The beer industry is one of the most highly regulated businesses in the United States and keeping on top of the myriad laws that govern the sales and marketing of alcohol beverages is critical. However, he also expects that I bring a sharp point of view to all elements of our business far beyond my functional role.

THE TELESCOPE AND THE MICROSCOPE

I use a metaphor with my team that I am sure I heard somewhere along the way. For us to be the best communications team, we must have one eye that's as focused as a *microscope* to deal with issues immediately in front of us, and one eye as focused as a *telescope* that looks out on the horizon to get in front of things that may become issues down the road. Our training as communications professionals typically is all geared towards the microscope part of the metaphor, fixing and addressing issues in the moment. But, we provide as much value, if not more so, when we help position the company to avoid issues in the future. In order to recognize what may or may not become an issue takes a keen understanding of the business your company is in.

PROBLEM-SOLVING REQUIRES COMMON UNDERSTANDING

As Stephen Covey has said, "seek first to understand, then to be understood" (Covey, 2004). That means that any professional must first build a deep understanding of whatever problem you may be trying to solve. Once you have that understanding, you can better frame your arguments to be better understood. Problem-solving will be better because everybody will have a common understanding of what the problem truly may be and the solutions can be debated from that common point.

I have persuasive debates with my colleagues in legal, finance, operations, HR, sales, and marketing on a daily basis. My arguments and positions often are framed by the communications, government, or community lens (as per my functional role), but they must be rooted in business rationale for my perspective to have impact.

As a college student or younger professional, I would encourage you to lean into your fears and shore up your weaknesses every chance you can, as uncomfortable at it may be initially. Luckily, there are more ways than ever to add to your skillset and knowledge base. At the most aggressive, there's the pursuit of an MBA. There are part-time and full-time programs and standard classes or online education opportunities where you can go at your own pace. You can pursue a certificate program at a local college or university in a specific topic, such as accounting or economics. You can buy books on certain topics or you can learn online in myriad ways through tutorial videos, classes, or lectures. You can seek out mentors or advisors who are subject-matter experts that can guide you to learn what is most relevant and informative. If you stay curious and always seek to get smarter, educational tools are more available than ever.

Whatever your appetite may be for advanced learning, there is a wealth of information at your fingertips waiting for you. How deep and wide you want to go is entirely up to you. What is certain is that you won't regret the chance to be smarter and more effective at your job, and you will benefit from it in many ways.

Career Spotlight

By Peter Marino, Chief Public Affairs and Communications Officer, MillerCoors, and President, Tenth and Blake Beer Company

What was your first job in communications?

I was an intern at Cramer-Krasselt, an integrated marketing agency in Milwaukee, Wisconsin. I was able to convert that internship into an Assistant Account Executive role after a few months.

What is a favorite career memory?

Starting and growing Dig Communications with a bunch of fun, smart, similar-minded folks who liked to challenge the status quo was just awesome. I loved everything about being an entrepreneur and disrupting the agency landscape in Chicago.

What is your career advice?

Bring a great attitude to work every day. Be aggressive, be aware, stay intellectually curious, and never be afraid to articulate your point of view. Don't be afraid to debate colleagues to make the outcome better. Never, ever be bashful!

REFERENCE

Covey, S. R. (2004). *The 7 habits of highly effective people: Powerful lessons in personal change.* New York, NY: Simon & Schuster.

4

FROM FARM TO PHARM: BUSINESS AND LIFE LESSONS LEARNED IN THE BARNYARD

Jeffrey A. Winton
Astellas Pharma

I was born and raised in a small farming town of 500 people in rural upstate New York, not far from Lake Erie. Like the majority of the people who lived in this area at that time, my family made their living in dairy farming.

Here are some lessons I learned while growing up on the family farm that have been instrumental in any success that I have achieved subsequently in the business world. While many of these lessons will seem like common sense, I would suggest that today's business world could benefit greatly from more *values-driven* common sense and behaviors.

LESSON #1: OTHERS ALWAYS COME FIRST, EVEN IF THEY ARE COWS

I am the oldest of four boys, and from the time that we could walk, we worked alongside our parents on that farm. Life on a dairy farm is a hard, 24 hour, 365 day a year job. The cows must be milked twice a day, and their needs were attended to before ours.

Because of the demands of the farm, many days the alarm clock would go off at 5:00 a.m., and we would go to the barn to feed and water the calves and milk the cows before going to school. Fortunately, our father was also our bus driver, so if he knew that we were running a tad behind in the morning chores, he would adjust the speed of the bus accordingly so that we weren't late for school.

LESSON #2. SLEEP IS HIGHLY OVERRATED, AND MULTI-TASKING WILL SERVE A COMMUNICATIONS PROFESSIONAL WELL

During certain times of year, we could be working until well past 10:00 p.m. at night, especially when crops were being planted and harvested. After farm chores were done, we would then do our homework, sometime finishing around midnight. Then, the clock would go off at 5:00 a.m. again, and the cycle would begin all over again.

LESSON #3: STAND UP, SPEAK UP, AND HELP THOSE WHO DON'T HAVE A VOICE

My family didn't have much money, but we always had what we needed. There were people much worse off in the area than my family, and my parents always made certain that they helped others; they taught us the importance and value of caring for those less fortunate.

LESSON #4: EDUCATION IS A GIFT THAT SHOULD NEVER BE TAKEN FOR GRANTED

My father was an extremely bright and accomplished business-man, despite the fact that he didn't have the privilege of going to college. About the time that my dad would have begun to think about college, my grandfather, who was also a farmer, became quite ill with polio. If my father had left to go to college, the family would have been forced to sell the farm, and so dad stayed behind and took over the family farm.

I was the first person in my family to attend college, and through hard work and frugal savings on my parents' part, I was given the opportunity to attend Cornell University where I studied agriculture. The older I get, the more I realize the tremendous sacrifices that the family made to send me to such a good university. Even though it was tough for them to get away from the farm, they visited when they could. Secretly, I do believe that my dad lived the college career he didn't get through my four years at Cornell. He especially seemed to enjoy the fraternity parties.

LESSON #5: NEVER UNDERESTIMATE THE POWER OF THE HUMAN SPIRIT

I began my career working in agricultural communications, where I had the opportunity to learn from some of the best minds in the business on Madison Avenue in New York City. I was specifically hired by the agency because of my farm upbringing and my agricultural degree. They agreed to teach me the communications field if I taught them about agriculture. That was my first glimpse into why having a grounding in business is important.

Back then, most pharmaceutical companies were also associated with crop chemical and animal health companies, so my clients represented a number of Fortune 500 companies. I eventually moved to the client side, and, over the course of my career, I moved into the human health area. My first job was working for a Swiss pharmaceutical company, handling patient advocacy and public affairs for their HIV/AIDS portfolio. Working directly with people living with this devastating disease was perhaps one of the most humbling and instructive positions that I have ever had.

LESSON #6: PEOPLE ARE PEOPLE AND HAVE THE SAME HOPES AND DREAMS, REGARDLESS OF WHERE THEY ARE BORN OR WHERE THEY LIVE

My current role involves leading all corporate affairs for Astellas Pharma, which is based in Tokyo, Japan. I have learned a great deal from my Japanese colleagues and their culture. In many ways, the Japanese work ethic is like the work ethic I learned while growing up on that rural dairy farm in upstate New York. The Japanese are very gracious people, who extend hospitality and warmth even in the business setting. They are also very loyal and dedicated to their work and their company, and they are committed to excellence in everything that they do.

LESSON #7: PURSUE YOUR PASSION AND DO SOMETHING WITH YOUR LIFE THAT MAKES YOU FEEL GOOD AND ENERGIZES YOU

Working in the pharmaceutical industry, especially for Astellas, a company that has a growing portfolio in oncology, I feel good about our work. Even at the end of a long and trying day, you feel that maybe, just maybe, you did something that helped advance the science that will be necessary to finally discover the cure for this dreaded disease.

I lost both of my grandmothers to cancer when they were in their early sixties, and I distinctly remember the valiant fight they fought. My grandmother Winton urged me to pursue a career in pharmacy (she didn't realize that chemistry was a living nightmare for me) when she was in her last days. My grandmother Wickstrom held on as long as she could in an attempt to see her first grandchild graduate from college, but sadly, she didn't quite make it.

Perhaps the biggest lesson of all that I learned on that hilly family farm in small town New York is that life is precious and fleeting, and there are no makeovers. We are placed on this earth for a finite period of time to make a difference and to help others. As communicators, it is our responsibility to tell this story.

LESSONS LEARNED ON THE FARM HELP NAVIGATE THE C-SUITE

I once had a CEO tell me that I was one of the few people in his organization that shared the good, the bad, and the ugly with him when we met. He said that most senior leaders only wanted to tell him the good news, but for him to be effective as the top leader of the organization, he especially needed to know when things *weren't going well*. On a farm, a person is dealing with life and death every day, and many days, there are many more things that go wrong than go right. This lesson has taught me to always be transparent and honest with the CEO, with other members of the C-suite, and with the teams that I lead. As communications professionals, we are exposed to many things in the organization, due to the span of our responsibilities, so it is important that these key developments be shared with other members of the C-suite, despite how painful they may be.

My farm upbringing also taught me that humility, gratitude, hard work, and perseverance are critical in the business setting, especially working with the C-suite. In the pharmaceutical industry, we are working fervently every day to find the next advancement in cancer care, the cure for HIV/AIDS, or a breakthrough in Alzheimer's disease. This mission is why we work in this industry, and why the senior leaders of our organizations have such high expectations of each person who steps foot into a pharma

C-suite View

By Jim Robinson, President, Astellas Americas

Now, more than ever, communications professionals play a critical role in helping to shape and deliver messaging necessary in today's policy and government setting. With a new administration in Washington, the pharmaceutical industry is listening and learning how to work most effectively with our newly elected government officials so we can ensure access to medicines for people who depend on them.

The values-driven common sense and behaviors that Jeff Winton learned as a young man growing up on his family's farm have been put to good use at Astellas. We formed a new Corporate Affairs organization a few years ago under Jeff's capable leadership that now brings together functions including corporate, business and employee communications, stakeholder engagement, policy and government affairs, corporate events, and corporate social responsibility.

The common thread between all of these teams is that they are the storytellers for our company, regardless of who their ultimate audience may be. As we face the many opportunities and challenges in our industry, it is critical we have a consistent and coherent narrative that can be tailor-made and utilized for everyone responsible for telling our story.

As Jeff references in his essay, at Astellas, we believe in putting others first — the patients who depend on our medicines. Our work in the Policy and Government Affairs area is dedicated to ensuring that medicines continue to be available for the patients who we serve. Our company is filled with passionate and committed people — whether they work in the C-suite, the research laboratory or our mailroom — who believe we are making a difference in patients' lives.

Career Spotlight

By Jeffrey Winton, Senior Vice President, Corporate Affairs, Astellas Pharma

What was your first job in communications?

My first job in communications was working for a Madison Avenue advertising and public relations agency. The agency specialized in human health clients, but they also had some agricultural clients. They liked my farm upbringing and college degree in agriculture, and they agreed to teach me the communications business if I helped them learn more about agriculture.

What is a favorite career memory?

My first job working in the human health business was serving as a patient advocate in the early days of the HIV and AIDS epidemic. I had the honor and privilege of representing the needs and voices of people living with AIDS inside the walls of a major, multinational pharmaceutical company. Very little was known about this horrendous disease in those days, and so every small advancement made was considered significant and potentially life-saving.

What is your career advice?

My late father gave me this career advice when I was contemplating leaving a job and people I loved for a seemingly better opportunity. He reminded me that one of the most important things about any job is the people with whom you work each day. He urged me to surround myself with positive, sincere, humble, genuine, and fun people. Because of his advice, I chose *not* to leave the job, and it was one of the best decisions of my career.

company as an employee. We have all been patients, and, sadly, we have all lost friends and family to the ravages of devastating diseases.

Checking your ego at the door is instrumental in our work. Farm kids learn very early in life that many things in life are completely out of your control. So when things *do* go right, you are thankful and you take nothing for granted, and when things go wrong, you realize that tomorrow is another day filled with possibility.

PART III

FINANCE AND INVESTOR RELATIONS

5

TAKING THE NUMB OUT OF NUMBERS: WORKING WITH THE OFFICE OF THE CFO

Kathryn Beiser[a,b]
[a]Edelman
[b]Hilton Worldwide

I think I was employee number five to get the news.

Coffee in hand, kids off to school and the traffic report on the radio, I had just gotten in my car to make the trek from Chicago to the suburbs where I was head of corporate communications at Discover Financial Services. My phone rang. It was my boss, which was highly unusual given the early hour. He asked how soon I could be at the office because he had some confidential information to share that required my help. I replied that it would likely take me another 30 minutes. He paused, and then said, "Good. We are spinning off from Morgan Stanley to become an independent, publicly traded company. We're going to get it done in six months so we need to start now. Only a few people know and you can't involve your team at this point. Come to my office as soon as you get in."

So began one of the most important assignments of my commu-nications career. Intense, exhausting, and exciting, the spin-off demanded that my team and I deliver our very best strategic think-ing and tactical implementation in support of a mission-critical objective. Along the way, we forged stronger bonds with our Chief Financial Officer (CFO) and the finance team, enabling us to develop a deeper understanding of the business and ulti-mately deliver better counsel once we were a public company. And for me personally, the experience taught me to love "the numbers" — a rather unexpected outcome for someone who had pursued a career in words and images, but one that fundamentally changed my perspective about corporate communications and added an important, fulfilling dimension to my career.

IT STARTS WITH THE FUNDAMENTALS

Don't get me wrong; I was no stranger to numbers. I just didn't like them for much of my career. I suffered through my economics and calculus classes as an undergrad. In graduate school, I was elated when we finally finished the module on "finance for non-financial managers." During the first 15 years of my career as a consultant, I worked on several financial transactions, dealt with some challenging regulatory situations, and wrote some quarterly earnings releases and an annual report, but I can't say those assignments were among my favorites at the time.

Turns out, though, that all that early education was critical preparation for my role as a chief communications officer. By learning to read a balance sheet, understanding the financial mar-kets, and comprehending the basics of corporate finance, I spoke the same language as my C-suite colleagues. Instead of having to learn the fundamentals of finance, I could focus immediately on communications strategy, which was critical given the tight dead-lines we were under at Discover. I distinctly remember during one of the early meetings about the spin-off — in a room filled with senior executives with deep financial expertise and experience — having a moment of revelation when I realized I understood everything that was being discussed. Okay, so maybe there were some nuances and technical details that gave me pause, but I recall thinking, "I've got this. And now I can do my job." At that point, I really started warming up to numbers.

C-suite View

By Roy Guthrie, Chief Financial Officer (retired), Discover Financial Services

For every Kathy Beiser who loves words, there's a Roy Guthrie who is intimidated by them. In fact, one of my greatest fears is a clean sheet of paper... unless it happens to be an empty spreadsheet. That's why I value my relationship with the communications department — our disciplines depend on each other to tell a complete story about an organization.

One fundamental thing I've learned in my career is that the audience for a company's financials is very diverse. Some people are quite sophisticated about the numbers, while others' eyes glaze over when the conversation turns to debt/equity ratios or asset turnover. The key is to understand the needs, strengths, and weaknesses of each audience, and surround the numbers with the appropriate level of context so we tell a compelling story.

And everyone needs at least a few numbers; data is critical to sizing the story. What does "a huge opportunity for our company" really mean without some information about the size of the market and the share of it that you intend to capture? It's not about overwhelming people with numbers, but rather finding the ones that tell the story best.

Working with finance isn't difficult if you have some basic knowledge about numbers and are prepared to ask plenty of questions. Remember: we need you as much as you need us.

Lesson learned: Do the hard work to understand the basics of finance. You'll thank yourself later.

NUMBERS NEED A STORYTELLER

Another call I received during those early days of the spin-off process was from Roy Guthrie, the CFO of Discover. He wanted to know if I would write the business description for the Form 10, which is the registration statement that the Securities and Exchange Commission (S.E.C.) requires a spin-off company to file before it can trade securities on U.S. exchanges. As a division at the time of a larger company, Morgan Stanley, we hadn't needed this kind of in-depth description before, so nothing existed that we could modify — we would be charting new territory. I had never written even a paragraph for an S.E.C. registration document, much less a substantive section, so I wasn't sure what I might be getting into. Roy assured me he could find someone else to handle this assignment if I was too busy. That's when I realized that I *had* to take on this assignment. Who else to craft the next chapter of Discover's story but the company's chief storyteller? Just because a Form 10 is a legal document with plenty of financial data didn't mean a lawyer or investment banker must write all of it.

While it took weeks of executive interviews, multiple drafts, and plenty of conversations with lawyers and investment bankers, we produced a thorough and objective description of Discover's credit card and electronics payments business. And we didn't just use words: for example, we realized that having some visual diagrams would be ideal for explaining how the Discover Network operated and how it interacted with the company's credit cards.

Telling a story about the numbers was something we also had to do with Discover employees. Understanding what it meant to be a public company and how we now had to follow different rules about reporting our financial performance required some changes for employees. We made sure that our communications department and all senior employees underwent training on the S.E.C.'s Regulation FD to ensure they understood the risks of selective disclosure. We also created plenty of Q&A documents, manager toolkits and articles on our company intranet to explain the spin-off process. And once we were public and reporting our numbers on a quarterly basis, we gave employees "plain English" communications about our performance that included plenty of visuals to help them understand our progress in greater depth.

Lesson learned: Numbers become more compelling with the right verbal and visual context that makes them real and relatable.

MAKING FRIENDS IN FINANCE

As a member of the Discover corporate communications function, part of my job was to connect with all departments within the company. One of my strongest relationships was with the finance team.

On a regular basis, I spent time with our CFO to better understand the business of our business, as well as get an idea of what might be happening next and why. Roy was always open to my questions, and frequently sought my perspective on how we might communicate various aspects of our financial position. I was fortunate, too, that Roy has a down-to-earth, clear approach to communicating — rarely did our rehearsals for quarterly Employee Town Hall meetings require much coaching to "keep it simple."

Another strong relationship I had within the finance organization was with our head of investor relations (IR). Through regular meetings, the occasional lunch and plenty of email traffic, I got an immediate, insider's view of what the Street was saying about our company and, very importantly, what messages were resonating

Career Spotlight

By Kathryn Beiser, formerly Global
Chair of the Corporate Practice,
Edelman, and formerly Executive Vice
President of Corporate
Communications, Hilton Worldwide

What was your first job in communications?

During my senior year in college, I worked in the PR department of Evanston Hospital. I still remember my first "hit" — Channel 7 in Chicago quoted my press release about the year's most popular baby names (I had noticed on the birth records that many were from the hit 1980s TV show "Dynasty").

What is a favorite career memory?

While I have worked on a lot of very serious and tough issues that were very satisfying experiences, it's the happy events that stand out the most. For example, I loved helping Discover celebrate its 25th anniversary — it was a year-long communications program rooted in authentic, strategic storytelling to internal and external stakeholders. Our strategy was to demonstrate how Discover's entrepreneurial, innovative beginnings were still very much part of the company's culture and driving its success. I had an amazing team and we had such fun planning and executing this initiative.

What is your career advice?

Pursue *learning* first — which can involve some detours — and *advancement* second. Each experience makes you a stronger, more substantive professional. If I had pursued a linear path, I might never have enjoyed such a satisfying career.

with them them...and which were not. These interactions helped my team and me better support our IR objectives through targeted communications to media and other stakeholders — the more accurate the overall context in which the financial community was receiving our messages, the greater the chance that our story would resonate with them.

Lesson learned: Find your "finance sherpas" who can help you navigate the ins and outs of your organization's business.

FINANCIALS FORM THE FOUNDATION

Whether working in agency or in-house leadership positions, I deal daily with numbers. No matter the business challenge, I rely on the financial knowledge and experience I gained earlier in my career, which enables me to have more robust, meaningful conversations with my clients and colleagues. There's a certainty and substance to numbers that provide a foothold for communicators — financials are the backbone of an organization, providing clues to its present and future. As W. E. B. Du Bois noted, "When you have mastered numbers, you will in fact no longer be reading numbers, any more than you read words when reading books. You will be reading meanings."

6

THE PARTNERSHIP BETWEEN CORPORATE COMMUNICATIONS AND INVESTOR RELATIONS

Carole Casto
Cummins Inc.

What do the Statue of Liberty, Mount Rushmore, Wrigley Field, and the expansive New Delhi Metro System all have in common? These three national treasures and one of the world's largest metro systems all rely upon backup power solutions from Cummins Inc.

The predecessor to Cummins Inc. was founded nearly a century ago by Clessie Cummins whose passion and expertise in engines helped win the first-ever Indianapolis 500. Today Cummins Inc. is a publicly traded, global power provider that designs, manufactures, distributes, and services diesel and natural gas engines and related technologies. Headquartered in Columbus, Indiana, Cummins employs over 55,000 people worldwide.

C-suite View

By Mark Smith, Vice President, Operations Finance, Cummins Inc.

At Cummins, collaboration between corporate communications and investor relations relies on trust and respect of one another's perspective, and finding balance between the two. Our partnership started years ago when, as the new leader of investor relations, I scrambled to have content reviewed by the group as an after-thought. Now, working with corporate communications is instinctual, leading to a proactive partnership with stronger, more effective communications across a range of topics and events, not just formal investor communications.

My role in the partnership provides a realistic, analytical perspective to longer-term business implications of an issue or opportunity to frame the correct context to communications. Corporate communications brings balance through developing consistent, clear messaging to our stakeholders, including 55,000 global employees, many of whom have joined Cummins within the last five years and may not understand the longer-term trends or competitive industry background. Upholding our credibility with all audiences requires us to be honest about the challenges we face, and enthusiastic about our successes.

This partnership also transformed communication to the larger finance function through technology. Corporate communications pushed our group to use live webcasts and videos to communicate with employees, and we received extremely positive feedback. We would be far less effective communicating to the larger employee base without corporate communications pushing us out of our comfort zone.

Ultimately, each groups' strengths yield highly effective messages to our global stakeholders, and, frankly, have driven deeper discussion of some challenges and opportunities within Cummins — and our company is better for it.

The corporate communications function at Cummins plays a unique role in advancing the company's strategies by providing professional communications services to all business segments and functions. Our team, comprised of external, internal, executive, visual, and digital communications professionals, collaborates with our customers — global partners and company leaders — to deliver creative and cost-effective communications solutions and services, including robust communication strategies, tactical support, and metrics.

These solutions and services help our customers achieve their business goals by setting clear expectations and objectives for our internal audience, inspiring employees, and educating our stakeholders about key corporate initiatives and projects. Based on the measured outcomes, we establish best practices and opportunities for improvement.

Although our corporate headquarters are located in Indiana, Cummins employees work in approximately 190 different countries and territories. While Cummins prides itself on diversity and global affiliations, it requires the organization to be multi-lingual and take into account vastly different time zones among our employee populations. Equally challenging for Cummins is the nearly 20,000 non-wired shop floor employees who do not have access to Cummins-provided cell phones and laptops.

Because of these unique challenges, we are constantly looking for ways in which business critical information, such as financial results, is shared more visually and creatively with our employees. Infographics are more easily consumed by a global workforce and can be presented on digital signage in order to reach our shop floor employees. These digital signage displays are located on the shop floor walls and present business-critical information using pictures that periodically rotate. Ultimately, by focusing on continuous improvement, corporate communications consistently adjusts how it supports customers to ensure they have the most effective strategies and tools at their disposal.

THE GROWTH OF A PARTNERSHIP

Corporate communications at Cummins has also evolved as a function to meet the demands of a complex and global audience by forming solid partnerships with other internal functions. One such function, investor relations (IR), is of great interest to all of Cummins' stakeholders, including the investment community. IR maintains the company's relationship with the investment community by communicating financial and business results, value drivers, strategy, and operations of the company. Over the last several years, corporate communications has grown to collaborate closely on all important IR initiatives to ensure financial messages are clear, accurate, and digestible by a global audience.

Three of these initiatives require especially close partnership:

Quarterly Earnings Release: Cummins releases financial results to its stakeholders on a quarterly basis, disclosing revenue, sales, outlook, and guidance. These quarterly earnings results are comprised of complex financial statements and language. To ensure effective delivery of these messages, IR works closely with corporate communications, beginning several weeks prior to the earnings release, assisting leadership with crafting messages for investors and our employees. By facilitating clear, concise, and consistent messaging at a corporate level, we are able to ensure that related messages to our employees from business segment leadership are aligned with overall corporate messaging to our stakeholders.

Annual Meeting of Shareholders: This annual event is attended by the Cummins board of directors, the Cummins leadership team and officers of the company. Immediately following the formal shareholder meeting, Cummins' Chairman and CEO delivers a keynote address highlighting the company's product launches, customer successes, and the important values-driven community work of the global workforce. Our team helps craft the key messages and visual stories to ensure the global audience can best understand the information. This exercise is helpful for leaders, too, as these stories can be repurposed and used throughout the year when addressing both internal and external audiences.

Analyst Day: Every two years, Cummins leadership meets in New York City with investment analysts from around the globe to share the company's plans to generate profitable growth and strong returns on capital. The analyst day meeting is designed to discuss both the company's response to current business conditions and our long-term plans for growth. This event requires close collaboration between corporate communications and IR to ensure appropriate and accurate language in describing Cummins' growth strategy. The presentation material created for this meeting is also used by our leaders to talk to internal and external audiences about growth over the coming years.

BUILDING BUSINESS ACUMEN IS A NECESSITY

Through these collaborative efforts, corporate communications has come to understand the importance of building business acumen within our function. More and more, customers encourage corporate communication professionals to attend their staff meetings, travel with company leaders to global locations for employee town hall meetings, and invite them to participate in discussions about critical business initiatives. This not only helps educate the communications professional, but allows him/her to identify opportunities to create consistent messaging across the company and to collaborate with other colleagues on company-wide communication events.

Moreover, the corporate communications function organizes continuing education opportunities on business concepts and strategy for our communication professionals, and actively seeks internal and external speakers on matters most important to the company and its growth strategies.

Ultimately, by continuing to provide creative, business-relevant communication expertise, and by continuing to increase our communication professionals' understanding of the business, corporate communications will remain a trusted advisor to not just the IR function, but to every segment, function, and leader in the company.

TIPS OF THE TRADE

Young professionals seeking a career in communications have a variety of opportunities to grow their skills in both the communication/PR and business space. Here are some tips of the trade:

1. *Be curious.* Learning never ends for the best communicators. Managers appreciate employees who are never satisfied with their current level of knowledge. Show enthusiasm for professional growth and appear eager for development opportunities.

2. *Grow your network.* Your peers will be some of your biggest allies along your career journey. Be sure to keep in touch with college classmates, colleagues, and anyone else who interests you professionally. These contacts can be counted on at almost any step of the way throughout your career by providing knowledge, answering questions, and helping you keep a pulse on happenings in your area of expertise.

3. *Keep an open mind.* Ask any vice president, executive director, or CEO where she thought she would be at age forty, and you'll find the answer usually does not mirror where she actually landed. Don't become discouraged if your path doesn't always appear linear, or you are offered a role that doesn't neatly align with your "perfect" career plan. Some of the best career opportunities come from where we least expect it.

Career Spotlight

By Carole Casto, Vice President,
Marketing and Communications,
Cummins Inc.

What was your first job in communications?

I was quite senior, serving as the Chief Operating Officer of the state of Indiana's environmental agency. Communications reported to me and the state's largest fish kill happened on our watch. I relocated my office to the scene of the crime and called daily and/or weekly press conferences. I am confident that the reoccurring drum beat of public accountability led to a speedy investigation and indictment.

What is a favorite career memory?

It's every time someone on my team promotes to a better opportunity! Developing people is rewarding work, and watching someone grow and excel is invigorating. As a leader, I enjoy nothing more than helping someone achieve their career dreams and provide a better life for themselves and their families.

What is your career advice?

Be more *interested* than *interesting*. You will learn a lot, satiate your curious nature, and you will get access to all kinds of interesting people, places, and opportunities. Pick important problems, fix them. One of my early mentors helped me to see the wisdom of this advice. Focus on the problems that will create the most impact for your organization. Dive in head first and hold yourself accountable. All of the great opportunities I have had are due to visibility that was created for me while I was fixing something that mattered.

Special thank you to Amy Yount and Meredith Whelchel of the Cummins Inc. Corporate Communications team for contributing to this chapter.

PART IV

HUMAN RESOURCES AND EMPLOYEE ENGAGEMENT

7

MASTERING BUSINESS MEANS FIRST UNDERSTANDING YOUR PEOPLE

Corey duBrowa[a,b]
[a]Salesforce
[b]Starbucks

For communicators, "business acumen" isn't just about mastering the nuts and bolts of a Profit and Loss statement. Instead, this phrase describes the outcomes that profitability drives for your business and the good this enables you to do in the communities in which you operate.

At Starbucks, running a profitable business is the price of admission; our "table stakes." This gives us the permission and the means to make a difference in the world and provide meaningful opportunities for our people, who now number more than 330,000 in 75 countries. Our profitability also allows Starbucks to drive a culture of innovation — our collective ability to see around corners, anticipate what's next and drive new ideas through our operations and along to our customers. These new ideas can range from a new mobile technology, introducing a product line or a differentiated approach to becoming an even better employer of choice. Running a responsible business also allows us to return profits back to our people and key stakeholders.

C-suite View

By Lucy Helm, Executive Vice President, General Counsel and Secretary/Interim leader, Chief Partner Officer, Starbucks

I have the distinct honor of leading Starbucks partner resources team, which supports the more than 330,000 partners around the world who proudly wear the Green Apron.

I call it an honor because our people are central to the success and future of the company. And, the way that we communicate and engage with our people is so critical to that success — from the programs we offer; to the stands we take on issues that are important to our people; to the way that we bring them along in the journey of the future of our company.

The partnership that our team has with global communications is key, as we aspire to look through the lens of our partners before we communicate externally. It's through that consideration that we are able to build trust and confidence with our people, who are our frontline ambassadors to our brand. If we exceed the expectations of our partners, they will exceed the expectations of our customers.

TRUE PARTNERS IN THE BUSINESS

Let's begin with some context: why does Starbucks call its employees "partners?" Since our employees at every level are shareholders in the company and share in the company's success through profit sharing and equity in the form of stock, they are partners in our success. Their collective commitment to delivering the highest levels of customer service, coffee expertise, and sense of community and connection is core to who we are and our differentiation in the marketplace.

More critically, it is through the lens of our partners that we make our decisions on strategy and how best to grow our business. Since its founding in 1971, Starbucks has recognized that building a great, enduring company requires being performance-driven through the lens of humanity. This means that we must strike the careful balance between profitability and investing in our people and the communities we serve. Sometimes we make decisions in the short term that may not drive immediate profits, but in the long term are consistent with our values and help cement customer affinity for our brand.

One example that comes to mind is a benefit that has served as a cornerstone of Starbucks culture — healthcare. We have ensured that our partners and their families have access to affordable comprehensive healthcare coverage since 1988 — before we were even a public company — and were proudly one of the first companies in the United States to offer this benefit to both part-time (those working at least 20 hours) and full-time employees.

During Starbucks transformation in 2008, Howard Schultz had returned as CEO and was pressured by major shareholders to end this benefit to cut costs, given that healthcare is one of the most significant line items in our operating budget. Howard refused to cut the benefit, telling shareholders that it would fundamentally "sap the culture" and the reservoir of trust we had built over many years with our partners. This people-first point of view has helped build and preserve the culture that is so fundamental to Starbucks business success. And I have personally seen examples of this behavior over and over again during my time with the company.

To put a finer point on it: of those customers surveyed monthly who say they are planning to return for another visit within a month, nearly 70% say the primary reason is *not* our coffee, our store designs, or our convenience. It is because of their connection with our people, and, more specifically, evidence that we are treating partners well and with respect. Before I was ever a partner,

I was a Starbucks customer, and I had built a trust relationship with one of my local store's partners: Mary. I knew she was studying to become a nurse, that her family was from Oregon, and that her role at Starbucks was helping her to realize her dream to eventually enter the healthcare industry and serve others. In turn, she knew who I was, my favorite beverage, and those of my family as well. So to perhaps put this personal dynamic into perspective, we are a $20 billion global business done five dollars at a time. As such, we are highly dependent on the value of human capital and the relationship equity we build with each of the 85 million customers who visit Starbucks weekly, worldwide.

APPLYING THE "PARTNER LENS"

The first question we ask during the planning stage for any new endeavor at Starbucks is *will this make our partners proud?* We already know that our partners are our most important asset: the frontline "face" of our brand, engaging daily with millions of customers in thousands of stores around the world. Years of experience tell us that if our partners are engaged in and support an idea, then our customers will embrace it as well.

Our partners are also a crucial resource for us to identify the issues we choose to address as a company. This can range from products that we should discontinue (our partners were the first to articulate that we should move away from artificial ingredients back in 2009) to controversial issues we should take head-on (our partners have opened our eyes to injustices around the world, ranging from marriage inequality over the past decade to the need to offer more choice in healthcare offerings in the summer of 2016). This "lens" helps us to thoughtfully choose from among the many issues we could embrace in any given year: those in which our partners are front and center are often the most compelling.

Starbucks launched its College Achievement Plan in partnership with Arizona State University because we heard from our partners that one of their top concerns was the cost of higher education. Making this education free of charge through ASU Online has been a major investment, but one that has already resulted in thousands of enrollees and prospective graduates. The inspiration for our Food Share program came from partners who encouraged us to find a way to help address both food waste and the increasing level of food insecurity in our country. Applying a "partner lens" results in stronger and more impactful programs that resonate because they are that much closer to home.

A DIFFERENT KIND OF COMPANY

In Starbucks nearly 25 years as a public company, we have strived to create a unique culture as a different kind of company. We're not necessarily better than others, but a company committed to its mission, values, and guiding principles that stands for something more than merely ringing a register every day. We help create opportunity for our people and the communities in which they live and work. Our aim is to achieve meaningful results that include — but go well beyond — traditional notions of shareholder value.

This ethos, to me, forms the backbone of advice that I frequently provide to aspiring communications professionals:

- Life is too short to work for a company that doesn't treat you well. Seek that kind of organization out. If you're not working for one now, make the change.

- Mission, values, and purpose are a great focusing mechanism for any person in any business. There are bound to be challenging days no matter whom you work for, in any industry; having a bigger sense of mission for your work will help you through the toughest of those days.

- The measure of a leader is less directly tied to their individual accomplishments than it is to the success of those they coach, mentor, and shape into future leaders. I learned this from a professor who also served as my mentor; if I am any kind of leader at all, it is because I was busy paying attention to what a terrific man and teacher he was, every minute I was around him.

Career Spotlight

By Corey duBrowa, Executive Vice President and Chief Communications Officer, Salesforce

What was your first job in communications?

My first communications internship was working my junior year of college for an advertising firm in Eugene, Oregon called "Adlib." I worked with a variety of different clients on relatively low-level, primarily advertising-related tasks.

What is a favorite career memory?

Without question, it was helping to conceive and execute the Starbucks + HBO "Concert For Valor" at the Washington Mall on Veterans Day, 2014. For more about the concert, see https://news.starbucks.com/news/the-concert-for-valor

What is your career advice?

"What you do speaks so loud that I cannot hear what you say."

— Ralph Waldo Emerson. As public relations professionals, the best communication we do every day is guided by the *behavior* our organizations exhibit, and the extent to which it matches our missions and values.

At the time of this writing, Corey duBrowa was Senior Vice President, Global Communications for Starbucks. He has since joined Salesforce as Executive Vice President and Chief Communications Officer.

8

EMPLOYEES AS DRIVERS OF CORPORATE BRAND AND REPUTATION

Paul Gerrard[a] and Angela Roberts[a,b]
[a]Blue Cross Blue Shield Association
[b]American Veterinary Medical Association

Not long ago, an organization's reputation was largely shaped by its advertising, press releases, and public messaging. Today, thanks to social media, employees and interested parties engage in public dialogue about everything from the organization's internal culture to its manufacturing practices. Consumers now expect peer-to-peer input about an organization's products or services when making buying decisions, even considering its environmental impact and general reputation amongst like-minded friends. In its 2016 Trust Barometer research, Edelman (2016) revealed that people find a company's employees to be more credible than its CEO, stating: "If you build trust with your employees, they'll say good things about you. And when they do, consumers will believe them" (p. 13).

All of this means that the power to shape reputation has shifted from an organization's leadership to its employees, customers, and anyone else who has a social media account. That's why it is increasingly important that your workforce go beyond being simply aware of or "engaged" in your CEO's corporate vision. Instead, your employees must personify it and help execute it. We are in an age in which this is expected of — and demanded by — *all* levels of our workforce. Millennials, in particular, are willing and ready to do their part to help shape and implement the corporate vision.

As such, it is critical that the Internal Communications function deeply understands the strategic imperatives of the overall organization. It is also critical that Internal Communications operates as a strategic business partner to Human Resources (HR), creating an intersection where employees are able to interact with the larger organization.

NUTS, BOLTS, AND CULTURE

To achieve a healthy dialogue with employees, Internal Communications and HR must align goals and resources. At the most basic level is the mechanics of informing your employees about policies, benefits, wellness, training, and education — the nuts and bolts of their employment. At the Blue Cross Blue Shield Association (BCBSA), we have developed a suite of tactics to better communicate with our employees. This includes specific communications vehicles we deploy: a tailored intranet site, weekly electronic news digests, and regular meetings for managers. We also developed an editorial calendar for news and announcements, and coordinated with each division to understand their upcoming initiatives, which ultimately generates a controlled cadence of news to employees.

C-suite View

By Maureen Cahill, Senior Vice President and Chief Human Resources Officer, Blue Cross Blue Shield Association

In my experience, one thing has been consistent and certain — *change*. Whether it's the issuance of new regulations that directly affect business operations or swings in competitive conditions that force organizations to re-organize and re-prioritize, leading through change is a core competence for business leaders in today's world. These changes spark the need for HR to optimize communication techniques to support shifting objectives and engage employees.

Core to an organization's ability to successfully navigate change is its ability to communicate the need for change. Employees are better prepared to get behind a change when they understand the *why* behind an expectation that they work differently, why their benefits are changing or why a strategy is shifting.

Strong internal communication professionals belong at the HR leadership table because they help HR to consider the collective impact of the messages targeted at employees. They provide context to the flurry of information that change brings, helping employees accept change more quickly. It is imperative that the most important messages employees receive are clear and cut through the volume of information they are expected to absorb. Change is hard for most people. If employees believe they have been listened to and communicated to often through multiple channels — and as transparently as possible during periods of change — that builds trust.

And trust builds strong brand ambassadors.

Developing this framework requires collaboration. Historically, anyone in the organization who wanted to share an announcement with employees could write and send an email to everyone without checks or approvals. One problem with this approach was the lack of a common email format, visual design, voice, or tone. Worse, employees received multiple emails a day from various disparate leaders or groups. If you wanted to re-read an announcement you had received, you had to remember who sent it. If you were behind in your emails, you missed important messages. Compounding these problems was the issue of email prominence: an announcement about a volunteer event held the same weight as an announcement from the CEO about an organizational restructure.

To create a better approach, Internal Communications (which, along with External Relations, Public Relations and Executive Communications, is part of the Strategic Communications function at BCBSA), first partnered with HR to craft a plan for improved communications, outlining the challenges and identifying solutions. We then met with various department leaders to understand their goals and broad initiatives, to explain why a coordinated, centralized approach to internal communications is critical, and to gain their buy-in.

Now, teams across the organization submit news to the Internal Communications team to be edited, proofread, formatted, and communicated in a timely and strategic manner. Additionally, employees have a single, weekly source for all news and announcements and can turn to the intranet site for more detail on various items.

Beyond the nuts and bolts, Internal Communications partnered with HR at a strategic level to refine and drive the culture of the organization. Recently, the HR team developed new tenets of employee standards called "Leadership Expectations" and "Employee Expectations." The Internal Communications team helped socialize these tools by introducing them at executive-led Town Halls, discussing them at quarterly managers meetings and providing employees with printed and electronic materials to reinforce them.

BEYOND YOUR WALLS

Your audience isn't just limited to your current employees. A less obvious audience is made up of the people who *want to* work for your organization.

Every organization has an employment brand. Which is to say, how do you describe your organization and its culture to prospective employees? How do you represent your culture on your website, and does it match what a person will find when they apply, come in for an interview, and/or are hired? Internal Communications works hand in hand with HR on recruitment materials, new hire orientation, messaging for college recruitment fairs, and more. Our Internal Communications team worked closely with HR to identify core messaging, write content for brochures, choose images that appropriately reflect our physical workspaces, and accurately describe the work that takes place here. Together, we ensure that whoever strives to work at BCBSA has a positive experience that aligns with our overall brand and boosts our reputation.

A third audience for BCBSA may be the least obvious of all. In fact, while you've most likely heard of Blue Cross and Blue Shield (BCBS), chances are you are not familiar with its unique structure. We are a federation of 36 independent health insurance companies located across the country. BCBSA is the association that unites them. Because of this unique structure, the employees of the 36 BCBS companies are another primary audience for BCBSA. And critical to our success is effective communications with them. One mechanism we use is an "extranet" site — a website created for, accessible by and restricted to the employees of the BCBS companies. Recently, we partnered with HR to create a section on that site, specifically for the HR professionals within the BCBS System, where they can share materials, best practices, and critical information.

PEARLS OF WISDOM

As the role of employees as brand ambassadors continues to grow (Edelman, 2016), so too will the worlds of Internal Communications and HR continue to merge. Learning how HR operates is not a mystery. Our advice: Sit down with leaders from the HR team and learn their goals and priorities. Then, don't just function as a service provider (by fulfilling requests for communications support), but consider the specific requests *within the context of everything else going on in the organization*. As a Communications team, we have the broadest view across the organization because we interact with every department. We have the ability — and the responsibility — to balance incoming requests against each other and, ultimately, weave together various initiatives, campaigns, and programs into a balanced cadence of employee dialogue. By doing so, the Communications team can transform itself from a basic service provider to a valuable consultant and, eventually, a primary driver of the CEO's corporate vision.

TEAMWORK

A final point is perhaps the most important: A great team is reliant on a collection of professionals who are willing to step forward to champion their area of expertise — as well as a leader who lets them do so by giving them the room to implement. As you join a team, get comfortable diving deeply into areas you're curious about. Take time to develop areas of interest and hone your skillset. Commit yourself to the mission of the team, thoughtfully raise your opinions, and confidently contribute your perspective. This kind of passion will carry you well into your career.

This is also true when it comes to working with other functions and departments. Effective coordination, collaboration, and integration require building a team of experts that can work fluidly

Career Spotlight

By Paul Gerrard, Vice President, Strategic Communications, Blue Cross Blue Shield Association

What was your first job in communications?

I was a research assistant to three members of the British Parliament (MPs). In this role, I researched and reviewed upcoming pieces of legislation; wrote political research briefs; and communicated with constituents and other stakeholders on behalf of the MPs.

What is a favorite career memory?

First, it has been those occasions when I have been part of a team that affected change through great communications. For example, through the development and execution of a multi-faceted advocacy campaign that changed the government's position on a major piece of legislation. Second, those occasions when I have been able to support a team member's career growth — either as a manager, mentor, or friend.

What is your career advice?

If you enjoy what you are doing, your chances of a successful career are multiplied — so take the time to develop areas of interest and hone your skillset. Also, commit yourself to the mission of the team, thoughtfully raise your opinions, and confidently contribute your perspective.

across the organization's business units. Just as today's HR model immerses HR Business Partners into specific business units who then can offer high level strategic consultation, so too is the Communications team becoming much more strategic in supporting that collaboration. Gone are the days of simply helping HR communicate the basics of benefits to employees. Today, the strength in our role is serving as internal business consultants, offering a two-way dialogue with employees, communicating the brand internally and externally, helping HR to attain and retain talent, and providing a conduit for your workforce to play a functional role in the CEO's corporate vision.

At the time of this writing, Angela Roberts was Managing Director of Strategic Communications at the Blue Cross Blue Shield Association. She has since joined the American Veterinary Medical Association as the Chief Marketing and Communications Officer.

REFERENCE

Edelman, Inc. (2016). *2016 Edelman Trust Barometer: Executive summary.* New York, NY: Edelman, Inc.

9

HAVE A SEAT AT THE TABLE — NOT ON THE FRINGES

Anne C. Toulouse
Boeing

I had never envisioned myself in an employee communications role, but once I found myself leading the Employee Communications organization for Boeing, I had to own it.

Until then, I had always gravitated toward public-facing positions. Now that I am back on the public-facing side as vice president of Global Brand Management for Boeing, and have had some time to reflect on the several years I supported Boeing Human Resources (HR), I can say that it was one of the hardest — and most gratifying — roles I have had.

GET SMART — AND GET HELP GETTING SMART

In a corporate environment, HR communications must closely align with and support the business objectives. The more understanding you have of the business, the better conversations you can have with the C-suite, or senior executives. And the more solutions you can bring to the table, the greater chance you will have to show a return on the company's investment in communications. Being informed and involved can make the difference between being perceived as an *expense* versus being seen as a *worthwhile investment.*

C-suite View

By Rick Stephens, Former Senior Vice President, Human Resources and Administration, Boeing

I held leadership roles in several major aerospace programs — including the Space Shuttle — prior to running Human Resources and Administration. I believe that leadership is about providing perspectives, influencing attitude and, ultimately, helping those on the team see the way forward the same way that I do. I always viewed Communications and those on the communications team as vital to success. When communicators come to the table as well-informed business partners, their efforts are a differentiator for an organization's success, particularly during times of change.

I set out to create an employee-focused Human Resources organization that would be a competitive advantage for Boeing. To this end, there were high expectations for the Communications team. As we worked on change initiatives, I expected them to anticipate employee concerns, listen at all levels of the organization, and share timely — and "unvarnished" — employee feedback. I also expected them to push back when necessary.

My Communications team met these expectations. At one point, we had to create a compelling business case for health care changes where few changes had ever been made. After the campaign, 80% of respondents said they understood why benefits were changing. This effort brought about the best possible outcome for the business and employees in a challenging situation.

Fortunately, I'm a naturally curious person. So when I jumped into the new role, I tapped into every resource I could think of to learn about HR priorities, such as health care benefits, well-being programs, pensions, and retirement plans. I talked with people inside the company, benchmarked other companies, consulted with experts, and read everything I could get my hands on. It struck me that to be successful I really needed to understand the role of the top HR executive, so I made friends with a book called *The Chief HR Officer*, by Patrick M. Wright. I was a communicator coming from a different role; how could I support a top executive if I didn't understand the organization? The Boeing senior vice president of HR at the time, Rick Stephens, and several of his HR leaders served as informal mentors, which I really appreciated. I made sure I attended the weekly HR leadership calls and monthly meetings. I immersed myself in all the topics, even if they didn't directly apply to my work, so I would be well-versed in all aspects of HR.

YOUR COMPANY HIRED YOU TO BE GREAT. BE GREAT. GET IN THERE!

It wasn't always easy. The HR team wasn't accustomed to seeing Communications as a partner, so I had to overcome some biases. Sometimes I had to really stick to my guns in order to be included. I did not miss a meeting. As Walt Whitman said, "We convince by our presence," so I was always there. Once there was a big strategic brainstorming meeting scheduled in the middle of my family vacation. I returned from vacation a day early so I could be at that meeting. When I arrived, I found that the meeting had started *an hour early* and nobody told me. I had to have thick skin and realize it wasn't personal. I took every opportunity to show what I could bring to the table. And over time, the HR team came to accept me as a partner.

Not only did I sit in on the HR leadership team, but I was also on the Communications leadership team, which gave me a chance to work with communicators in the business units, finance, government operations, and other organizations. That helped me maintain a 360-degree view of what was going on across the company, throughout our industry and in key markets. That knowledge strengthened my value as a contributing colleague.

IT'S ALL ABOUT YOUR AUDIENCE

Given the overarching objectives of the Human Resources organization — to motivate, engage, and inspire employees — Communications partners have to be able to simplify, clarify, and crystallize complex topics so that employees understand them. We are not asking employees to become subject-matter experts in health care, pensions, or retirement plans, but we have to give them the information they need to make informed decisions. So it is helpful for Communications to be at the table when HR programs are being developed and to bring a communications point of view toward what a program needs to be successful.

One big challenge we faced, in which it proved critical to engage Communications early, involved upcoming changes to the pension plan. Boeing's plan ranked as the largest among all U.S.-based corporate pension plans, posing a significant competitive disadvantage. Changes had to be made for the health of the company — but any changes would have to be communicated to employees carefully.

The HR executive gave me a heads-up months before communications would begin, so I had a chance to do research and advance planning. My team and I spent a lot of time benchmarking other companies, asking them to share their lessons learned. Based on our research, we knew that we had to communicate in a way that put the employee first. We had to anticipate where risks might lie and mitigate them. Because the plan involved closing the several different pension systems and moving employees to a 401(k)-type plan, we were addressing a huge population and facing a complex task. I centered the work on the idea that everyone matters. Even when we were dealing with a small population on a particular pension plan, that's the philosophy we held to: *Everyone matters*, and communications must be employee-centric.

I advocated for offering financial counseling to employees and providing them with tools, such as a pension calculator, so they could understand the changes. We were able to condition the environment so employees understood the reasons behind the change, even if they weren't happy about it. A majority of employees used the resources we provided, and many expressed their appreciation to leaders for listening to their concerns. The communication effort became a model for subsequent benefits program changes.

WHAT I WISH I HAD KNOWN FROM THE BEGINNING

Ultimately, by having an approach that was deeply rooted in the business objectives, by being fairly knowledgeable about the topic, and by having gained the HR organization's confidence, I was able to be at the table and have those conversations with HR that led to our mutual success. I think these lessons may be helpful for anyone entering a new assignment:

- Find informal or formal mentors who can help you understand the nuances, politics, and operating rhythm of the organization you are supporting. There are subtleties in each organization's culture that aren't visible from an organizational chart.

- Conduct research and study in the field on your own and with guidance from your mentors. Pull deep knowledge. You don't have to become a subject-matter expert, but you should be knowledgeable enough to carry on a conversation about the field. There isn't anything more impactful than being able to say: "I was just reading ..." or "I just talked to ...."

Career Spotlight

By Anne Toulouse, Vice President, Global Brand Management and Advertising, Boeing

What was your first job in communications?

I began my communications career as a civilian writer-editor for the Morale, Welfare and Recreation Division at Patrick Air Force Base, Fla. As the first person assigned to that role, I embraced the opportunity to develop a consolidated marketing program for a dozen recreation-oriented organizations. The Air Force work culture, based on giving people responsibility up front and trusting them to do the job, gave me an excellent foundation for later career success.

What is a favorite career memory?

One of the highlights of my career was working with Apollo astronaut Pete Conrad on an experimental rocket test in tough conditions: 90-degree-plus temperatures, sidewinder snakes, and minimal facilities. The hardships made the project into a shared "adventure" and helped to build strong working relationships. During a launch delay, Pete took me to a demolition derby and diner where he shared his stories of early space exploration.

What is your career advice?

Being intellectually curious and authentic can give you a competitive advantage in communications. You'll bring more value to your business partners as you demonstrate understanding of their goals, connect dots others don't see, and stay ahead of trends and opportunities. Being yourself will drive credibility and build your reputation — both of which are critical for long-term success.

• Volunteer to go to meetings and take on special projects. Make the most of every opportunity. Every meeting you attend, every connection you make builds your and your team's credibility.

- Before making recommendations or solutions, test them out on people who have experience. After you've made a presentation or have brought a solution forward, go to someone you trust and ask for coaching and feedback. Then apply what you've learned the next time.

- Ask a lot of questions, and then actively listen. I've relied on the Stephen Covey premise: "Seek first to understand, then to be understood."

Be informed, be involved, and you will become a valued member of the team you are supporting instead of lingering on the fringes. You will be more effective as a communicator and your job will be more satisfying, even when it takes you in directions you never envisioned.

PART V

CORPORATE STRATEGY, INNOVATION, AND LEGAL

10

COLLABORATING WITH STRATEGY AND INNOVATION: TAKING ON THE CHALLENGE TO "COMMUNICATE THE AMOEBA"

Linda Rutherford
Southwest Airlines

When I made the career move from journalism to communications, it took a while to understand that Communication — with a capital C — was about more than just the nuts and bolts of the information; about more than the five "w's" and the "h"; about more than just a clear writing style. Effective communication is a marriage between *the information* and *the understanding*. To get there, I had to understand what made the business work, how we made money, and what went into a strong financial reputation. Why?

FIRST STEP: WHAT'S IN IT FOR ME?

Because I had to connect the day-to-day purpose of Southwest — to connect people to what's important in our passengers' lives via air travel — to what's important in the lives of our employees. I had to help employees understand the financials, our priorities, and the competitive landscape to gain understanding of the higher meaning of their daily work. Communications professionals can "get smart" on these topics in a number of ways: take time to read the organization's financial statements and earnings reports; find a young professional in that department and see if they are willing to do an informal exchange of knowledge; seek a mentor to help you grasp complex topics in your industry and better understand them; and, lastly, you can always take a business class or read business books to enlighten you on different business terms or industry challenges.

For instance: we could just "communicate" the news of a policy change. We could simply issue a memo about a new destination or the company's decision to fly internationally. But, we had to take it further and subscribe to "what's in it for me?" Why should employees want to give incremental effort? Why should employees lean in and work hard to serve our customers? Why is getting that luggage to its intended destination or helping a customer comprehend a travel policy important to our bottom line?

As I have learned, it is important that the intended audience not only *understand the news*, but *see themselves in it*. So, it's about more than just putting a comma in the right place; it's about understanding the business and how it makes money to turn around and communicate something to a group of employees that will help them be educated, inspired, and engaged. Understanding leads to engagement.

COMMUNICATING THE AMOEBA

Enter the tough assignment. Tom Nealon, then Southwest's Executive Vice President of Strategy & Innovation and now our President, said to me one day: "Hey, would you help me communicate the new strategy? We need our employees to buy in to how we become the world's most loved, most flown and most profitable airline."

What I heard was more like: "How do you want to communicate this amoeba?"

Sometimes we get the awesome assignment to: communicate the amoeba.

We enter this profession with good training on what goes into basic communications — anything from news releases, internal communications, and magazine/online features, to communications plans and sometimes even speeches and presentations. But what Tom wanted was to take our aspiration to be the world's "most, most, most" and make it real, real, real for our employees. We had to take the big, hairy, audacious goal, and break it down and make it real for our employees.

So, our strategy — the multi-year roadmap to achieve our vision — was broken down into five major pillars. I would like to tell you this came from an academic learning somewhere along the way, but it was both on the job training and an observation of people that came in handy. Our team had decided that the best way to make the strategy real was first to get our employees interested in the messenger; once they were engaged and intrigued by Tom, they would listen to what he had to say.

MAKING THE BIG, HAIRY, AUDACIOUS GOAL REAL

The strategy overall is a path to "say yes" to the important things that would move us toward our vision and to "say no" to distractions. It would help us align the right resources to the right tasks. We began working to introduce Tom — an executive who our employees needed to know better — to our employees.

Tom listened to our advice. He intuitively understood that our people needed to know him in order to know his passion

C-suite View

By Tom Nealon, President, Southwest Airlines

The success of a 50,000-plus employee airline adopting a single corporate strategy depends on each employee knowing the *what*, *why*, and *how*. Getting that information to more than 100 locations, and to employees who are in constant motion throughout the day with limited discretionary time to read about something like a corporate strategy, is a daunting task.

Communicating a clear message to our employees in a way that they can relate to, and in a manner that cuts through the day-to-day demands on their time and attention, means we are deploying several different methods of communication that our Chief Communications Officer (CCO) hosts or influences across our company.

While I view communication as the responsibility of every leader at Southwest, I need the CCO and her team to amplify and position the messages in the right way. Gone are the days when a leader could walk out to the company gathering place and effectively communicate a single message to everyone at once. I talk a lot about the impact of a clear corporate strategy being one that will help us align the right resources to the right tasks. I feel the same is true of a clear communication strategy.

for helping the airline meet its objectives and achieve the mission to be the world's most loved, most flown, and most profitable airline.

During a leadership forum, Tom told the story about his upbringing and his collegiate soccer career. He was creating a parallel between building his skills as an athlete and how Southwest needed to keep its skills sharp — not be good at just one sport, but have aspirations to be a triathlete. Good at more than one thing at a time. Because that is what it would take for us to continue to be successful against a growing competitive landscape.

We took the five pillars — to protect our core business, empower our employees and strengthen our culture, control our costs, enhance the customer experience, and ensure reliable operations — and began breaking down what that would look like in the day-to-day operations. Southwest's Chairman and CEO Gary Kelly issues a "battle plan" letter each Fall and we included how the strategy would translate into daily activities.

Tom also needed help with visuals. We used our team to help him visually depict the five strategies literally as the number 5 — as in the five ways we will win. He started with a triangle, but we changed his mind based on the unintended but perceived importance of what was at the top of the triangle as the "tip of the spear" and, arguably, for what was at the bottom of the triangle as the "foundation" for the strategy.

During the annual employee rallies — hosted each February — our plan is to have Tom give his version of a "Ted Talk" to bring the strategy alive. We have created a "takeaway" item for each employee to help them keep the pillars top of mind. Lastly, we put metrics behind each pillar and created incentives (which we call Kick Tail goals) so when our employees come together to meet a goal, they get cash prizes or points in our incentive program. This will be an ongoing effort.

If an organization is to keep its strategy or spirit of innovation/continuous improvement top of mind for its employees, it needs to find omni-channel ways to keep it in front of its key audience in ways that keep it real for the audience. As a communications professional, you can:

- Help strategists make the link to real life: drive for desired behaviors and outcomes to come through in the communication. The strategy is X, but we need you to *do* Y.

Career Spotlight

By Linda Rutherford, Senior Vice President and Chief Communications Officer, Southwest Airlines

What was your first job in communications?

I had a post-graduate internship at *Newsweek* magazine in New York City. I met several people I still keep in touch with to this day, and the internship was a terrific way to explore what I loved most about communication and journalism. I learned it was the first person accounts — really being part of the action and then telling the story of what I saw or learned.

What is a favorite career memory?

It's not a happy memory, but one where I learned the most: December 8, 2005. My airline experienced its first accident with a fatality (a plane landing in a Chicago snowstorm overran the runway and landed on a car, killing a six-year-old boy). That put all my communications learnings to the test, taught me how dynamic and flexible our plans need to be, and how important it is to humanize even the most complicated issues and events.

What is your career advice?

- *See a need, fill a need.* Do whatever it takes as those opportunities are when you will learn the most.

- *Listen more.* Resist the need to show people how smart you are; they will appreciate you more when they know you are listening.

- *Don't take yourself too seriously.*

- *Have a perspective and share it.*

- Use personal stories to drive home relevance. Example: wearing seat belts is the law. Telling the story through one man's survival of an accident because he was wearing his has more impact and is a better way to illustrate cause and effect.

- Help bring the roadmap, strategy, or business plan to life with compelling visuals, video, and other collateral material so the audience can see themselves in the message.

And in the end: Less amoeba; more sophisticated organism.

11

TELLING THE STORY OF VALUE CREATION

Clarkson Hine
Beam Suntory

Nearly every day brings news of a major acquisition.

Behind each of these headlines is months of planning and cross-functional coordination, with the partnership between the leaders of the communications and strategy functions central to perceptions that can move markets, motivate people, and impact reputation.

WHAT STRATEGY DOES

At its core, the strategy function is about value creation. Companies create value in numerous ways, and buying and selling brands or business units can be among the most important decisions made by chief executives. Transactions are commonly developed by the corporate strategy function, which is responsible for identifying the universe of potential deals, and determining strategic fit, the upside opportunity and downside risk, and valuation. Not having a business or finance background, I had no idea what terms like synergies, enterprise value, or debt-to-EBITDA ratios meant when I started. So, I got "Street wise" through my responsibility for financial communications, and through close collaboration with our head of investor relations, chief strategy officer, CFO, and our CEO. Watching a lot of CNBC helped, too.

Transactions can range from "bolt-on" acquisitions to joint ventures to transformational mergers and unsolicited approaches. Companies continuously evaluate their own mix of brands and/or businesses. These portfolio evaluations may lead to asset sales, such as so-called "tail brands" or brands that are more valuable to another company than your own. Indeed, in 2016, our company enhanced its growth profile by selling several non-strategic brands, acquiring a fast growing super-premium brand, and investing in development of new growth platforms. Buyers and sellers are commonly advised by investment banks, and deals can be initiated by either side. While banks may run a formal sale process, deals can also begin informally. For example, our company recently acquired a brand after our chief strategy officer approached the brand owners by sending a message on LinkedIn.

Structuring transactions can be very complicated, and the process always relies on significant collaboration with the legal team. It is not uncommon for multiple opportunities to be under review at one time, and sometimes the best deals are the ones you *don't make*.

The value-creation remit of the strategy team extends far beyond deal making. Among the most important responsibilities of this team at our company is development of the three-year strategic plan, which serves as the roadmap for our mid-term growth. The "strat plan" identifies the internal sources of growth — including brands, innovation, markets, and channels — as well as potential merger and acquisition (M&A) activity.

C-suite View

By Steve Fechheimer, Former Senior Vice President and Chief Strategy Officer, Beam Suntory

From my perspective as our company's Chief Strategy Officer, ongoing partnership with the communications team is essential. One example is with merger and acquisition (M&A) activity, where I engage the communications function early for three reasons.

First, effective communications during an auction process helps provide an intangible edge. When I develop a purchase offer, I include narrative about why we would be the most suitable buyer of the brand or business. Companies want to be acquired by a company with a strong cultural fit and common heritage, and I'll rely on our Chief Communications Officer (CCO) to tell our story and develop the messages that will resonate with the seller.

Second, I rely on the CCO to ensure we are prepared if news of a potential deal leaks. Having proper statements prepared to deal with different situations is essential to being able to act quickly to save a deal.

Finally, some transactions entail important reputational issues, especially related to the prospect of facilities consolidations, layoffs, and the impact on local communities. Involving the communications team early enables us to analyze the reputational implications of a transaction, and develop the right communications to address all key stakeholders and help minimize risk.

At the time of this writing, Steve Fechheimer was SVP and chief strategy officer for Beam Suntory. He has since been named the CEO of New Belgium Brewing.

HOW WE WORK TOGETHER

Few corporate actions touch a wider array of stakeholders than M&A activity. So when it comes to a major strategic move, it is imperative for the chief communications officer to work collaboratively across multiple key functions, including with strategy, legal, HR, finance, and the CEO. This seat at the table helps ensure that the reputational implications and potential risks of a strategic move across stakeholder groups are evaluated early in the process. For example, a deal's cost synergies, such as layoffs or facilities consolidation, will be perceived very differently on Wall Street than by employees. Collaboration at the front end also helps ensure appropriate advance planning of any major announcement. When our company was evaluating the offer from Suntory Holdings in late 2013, a core internal group of just five senior executives, led by our CEO, managed the process for two solid months along with our investment bankers, outside counsel and the board of directors.

To help preserve the confidentiality of this project, which is critically important for a public company subject to strict securities regulations, we set up secondary private email accounts that could not be viewed by administrative assistants, often met off-hours and on weekends, and always referred to the project by its code name. Being a trusted part of this core group gave me intimate knowledge of the transaction and the strategy underlying it, and enabled development and delivery of a comprehensive communications plan with sharp messages for discrete stakeholder groups and plans for various contingencies. The collaboration and thorough preparation contributed to a highly successful announcement that helped build excitement and understanding among employees and customers for the new company, its ownership, and future prospects. This announcement also helped build support in the communities in which we operate, and helped demonstrate to the financial community the creation of shareholder value. Indeed, this announcement was front-page news in the *Wall Street Journal* and an introductory press conference in Tokyo was attended by 228 journalists.

The announcement of a major transaction is not the end to the cross-functional collaboration; it's really just the beginning. A significant business combination requires a carefully planned and executed integration. For the integration of Beam and Suntory, we established a project management office (PMO) structure with 25 separate workstreams to guide the commercial, organizational, and cultural aspects of the merger. We estimated that this process consumed more than 40,000 man hours in the first year alone. From my perspective, every minute of time I formerly spent on financial communications was quickly consumed by internal communications to help us build a common high-performance culture. There are numerous employee sensitivities in any acquired company, starting with the question: What does it mean for me? Naturally, it is critical for the CCO to be aware of the employee impact up front and plan communications accordingly. As important as amplifying a deal's value creation is demonstrating that a company is guided by its values.

In the acquisition of Beam by Suntory, we didn't foresee layoffs, but our people were rightfully curious and anxious about a new owner that many had not heard much about. That's why we made continuity and strong cultural fit two of our key internal messages, starting with our first communication on Day 1. We were gratified that our biennial employee survey showed that employee engagement actually *rose* during a time of change.

At our heart, communicators are storytellers, and the opportunity to bring corporate strategy to life goes straight to the core mission of any company — the story of value creation.

If you want to get more "Street smart," here are a few ideas:

• Review presentations from investor conferences, for your own company and your competitive set. It's instructive to see how other companies tell their stories to the investment community. These presentations, as well as archived webcasts of quarterly earnings calls, are commonly found in the investor section of company websites.

Career Spotlight

By Clarkson Hine, Senior Vice President, Corporate Communications and Public Affairs, Beam Suntory

What was your first job in communications?

In my freshman year at Cornell University, I joined the sports department at the student-run radio station. Working in radio taught me to write clearly, concisely, and quickly. I eventually became sports director, giving me early management responsibility. Combining radio with a passion for politics served me well in my first paying communications job as the head of radio services for Republican U.S. Senators.

What is a favorite career memory?

It's hard to choose, but one particularly fond memory is the reputation campaign I led at Fortune Brands during 2007–2008 to position our company to be the logical buyer of the iconic Swedish asset ABSOLUT vodka. It enabled me to use my entire toolkit and gain valuable international experience as we influenced perceptions through PR and public affairs in a highly competitive auction process (in which we were ultimately outbid).

What is your career advice?

(1) Consider starting your career in Washington. You can earn a lot of responsibility at a young age, and the communications skills required in politics translate well to business.

(2) Put a premium on writing — your own and when you hire. There are not enough good writers in the world, and you want to be your company's subject matter expert here.

(3) Know your business. You can't be an enterprise-wide leader without it.

- Read reports from securities analysts who cover your company and sector. Beyond the "buy," "sell," or "hold" recommendations, you can learn a lot about competitors and their strategies from these reports, and about how the Street perceives your own story.

- Review your own company's strategic plan and any internal competitive analysis, if you're in a position to request them. Any internal materials that demonstrate how your management sees the marketplace, now and in the future, can be very insightful.

- Watch business news channel CNBC. You'll hear a lot of different voices — including CEOs, analysts, fund managers, and business reporters — and you'll pick up the language of Wall Street quickly.

12

LESSONS FROM MY FATHER: BRINGING THE "GREENER RULES" TO CORPORATE STRATEGY AND PLANNING

Chuck Greener
Walgreens Boots Alliance

My father, William I. Greener, Jr., had a terrific career in public affairs. A retired Air Force colonel, he served as Jerry Ford's 1976 presidential campaign spokesman, President Ford's deputy press secretary, and Pentagon spokesman and communications chief for Donald Rumsfeld in his first stint as U.S. defense secretary. For his honest, straightforward way of dealing with a tough media, the Pentagon press corps ranked my father as the most effective spokesman since World War II began. He also headed communications for the pharma company G. D. Searles and held other high-level roles.

Along the way, my father developed a series of principles for corporate communications, known as "Greener's Rules." I knew about the rules from childhood because my father would practice his speeches in front of the family. In my own career in communications, his rules — honed and expanded with my own lessons learned — have been invaluable as I've sought to guide corporate decisions for the best long-term public outcome. I've been fortunate to have the opportunity to apply and hone these rules in my work for Fannie Mae and now for Walgreens Boots Alliance.

C-suite View

By Stephen B. Ashley, Former Chairman of the Board, Fannie Mae (FNMA) and Chairman, Chief Executive Officer and founder of The Ashley Companies

My time leading Fannie Mae's board of directors from 2004 to 2008 was a period of extraordinary challenge and crisis for the U.S. housing market and the company, which funds and underpins the market. Fannie Mae and our chief competitor, Freddie Mac, were under intense scrutiny and pressure from all fronts — the market, government regulators, shareholders, investors, Congress and the White House, the media and more. Fully involving our external affairs chief, Chuck Greener, as the Board and management worked through our strategy, was indispensable as he applied his father's "Greener Rules" to help keep our ship on course in rough seas.

As we dealt with this crisis, Chuck provided a crucial "inside-outsider's" view to the Fannie Mae Board and management. For example, when under harsh media scrutiny, it's natural to get defensive and want to strike back. Chuck helped us avoid the distraction and wasted effort, and stay focused on the real challenge: To support the housing market. Moreover, Chuck's role in coordinating communications between the Board chairman and the CEO enabled the two separate positions to work effectively together toward a consistent approach to the issues, internally and publicly.

All organizations should make their communications chief part of the boardroom and C-suite strategy, discussions, and decisions to ensure they are solid, sustainable and make sense to shareholders, stakeholders, and the public at large.

Here they are:

RULE #1: "MAKE SURE YOUR ASSUMPTIONS ARE RIGHT"

Communicators need to serve as internal truth-tellers — operating as the "inside reporter" — to test a company's assumptions, ask tough questions, and even raise uncomfortable issues. Keep pushing if the answer is unsatisfactory. Make sure you know everything. Ferret out the true story. Only then you can offer your best counsel and develop the best way to communicate it.

I have dealt with firms that wanted me to sell their internal spin on challenging situations they all face. My best service was: Let's start with the facts, unspin the spin, accept the truth, set forth the remedies if needed, and move ahead.

RULE #2: "YOU CANNOT CREATE AN IMAGE"

As my father said, images by definition reflect reality. To that I would add, "Good facts make good stories." By the same coin, you can't turn bad facts into good stories, but only try to minimize the damage and move out of the news cycle. Beware if management has bad news and says, "The key to this is going to be getting our message right." Or, instead of facing facts, they say, "Here's how you need to think about this."

The real key is to avoid being combative and defensive. As the *Chicago Tribune* reported about my father, "In the White House, Greener approved the [Ford] administration's relations with the press by citing what became known as 'Greener's Law' — 'never argue with a man who buys ink by the barrel' — to persuade Ford and other senior officials not to overreact to critical editorials or news reports."

At one company I knew well, a major national newspaper was developing a piece about how the firm was using a questionable financial instrument. Management was outraged by the claim, wanted to declare it was categorically untrue, and hit back. But unless the company could demonstrate the claim was untrue "without exceptions or conditions; absolute; unqualified and unconditional," as the dictionary defines *categorical*, the pushback could backfire. Attacking the publication would have only resulted in greater damage to the company's reputation.

RULE #3: "DON'T CONFUSE THREE YARDS WITH A CLOUD OF DUST"

Referring to the ground strategy of the legendary Ohio State football coach Woody Hayes, my father warned against confusing motion with progress. When a company faces a tough story, communications comes under pressure to react, to do *something*, sometimes to make people internally feel better — you're defending them — rather than doing nothing. But sometimes the best advice is, "Don't just do something — stand there" when reacting just keeps the story going.

Here's where corporate communications is different than political communications. In a political campaign, where you have a single opponent, they hit. You hit back. But there's a distinct end point: The election. The fight is over. The winner won. In the corporate world, the goal is building long-term reputation and value, so you're telling a long-term story. Reacting in the short run can be the cloud of dust that hurts the goal you're driving to.

RULE #4: "THINGS THAT GET MEASURED GET BETTER"

Long before today's Big Data and analysis, my father urged more time spent on measuring impact, and *measuring the right things*. My corollary: "It's all about accountability."

To illustrate, when a company is deciding its strategy, everyone wants a seat at the table. Communications needs a seat to make sure the strategy makes sense so it can be communicated internally and externally, so in the end you're not handed a pile of lemons to make lemonade. But communications has to *earn* that seat. The price is being accountable for our counsel. Today we have reputation metrics, tracking, dashboards, and other tools to measure the effectiveness of communications strategy. Management needs that measure not just to trust your counsel, but also gauge return on investment in communications.

RULE #5: "WE SERVE AS THE CONNECTING TISSUE"

In my father's day, public relations shops often were seen as merely order takers — an idea my father resoundingly rejected — where management made decisions and then handed off to communications to promote them. With today's glaring scrutiny — intensified by viral media — companies need to see communications as core to *decision-making*. Giving communicators a seat at the decision-making table can bring clarity, connection, and consensus to management decisions — and make sure they make sense to the outside world before launch.

One critical connection tool is often undervalued: Writing. When making big decisions, management sometimes believes everyone at the table shares the same facts and assumptions, and the strategy makes sense to everyone. It looks and sounds good in the presentations. But when the strategy is written out, and everyone reviews it, the process falls apart, the strategy doesn't make sense and you see there's not common understanding. One company I know developed a corporate reorganization plan that was brilliant — until it came time to communicate it with the business units and employees. In writing the announcements, gaping holes emerged in how people would be affected and the questions they would have.

RULE #6: "MAKE SURE YOU KNOW WHAT YOU ARE FIGHTING FOR"

Before companies move forward with a strategy or decision that will go public, ask a dumb question: What are we seeking to accomplish? It's incredible how many times companies head into an announcement, or even a fight, and enlist communications help without understanding the true goal. In a fight, management sometimes focuses on what the company is *against* versus what it is *for*. But you cannot win without something to play for. Every fight is a new chance to tell the world who you are and what you stand for.

RULE #7: "A LOT OF HUMILITY NEVER HURT"

Communicators always are on the front lines of corporate battles. In the heat of the fight, strong egos emerge. But ego can undermine success. For example, it's natural to assume nefarious intent when a reporter, a competitor, a regulator, or an activist is coming after you. But every story involves more than what we hear or assume. If we put ourselves in the other party's mindset, and call on our humility, we can come to a greater understanding of any situation and then deal with it better.

Along with humility comes a sense of humor. This is my father's best lesson. He did have fun. As the *Chicago Tribune* reported in 1985, "During an overseas presidential flight, Greener pulled a prank on *New York Times* correspondent Jim Naughton by suggesting that one of the celebrated bores of the press corps give Naughton an exclusive briefing on a visit to the plane's cockpit. After suffering a 45-minute briefing, Naughton later got even with Greener on a trip to Cleveland by placing a live rooster in his hotel room."

As New York magazine quoted Steve Martin in 1977, "You have to laugh once a day. Because a day without laughter is like night" (Coleman, 1977). Corporate communications is *not*, as cynics say, about spin, but expecting, planning for, and helping companies ride out the bumps that come with blazing new trails, stay on track and move ahead. My father might be stunned by the Twitter-paced news business today, but his insight and humor are timeless and still helpful and inspiring.

Career Spotlight

By Chuck Greener, Senior Vice President, Global Corporate Affairs and Communications, Walgreens Boots Alliance

What was your first job in communications?

Aside from my first post-college stint doing political research at the Republican National Committee for the 1976 presidential campaign, at age 23, I managed my first U.S. Congressional campaign helping to elect former House Rep. Bill Gradison from Cincinnati. While not specifically a communications job, the role required a great deal of communications including outreach to voters, campaign supporters, the community and, of course, the media.

What is a favorite career memory?

I've been very blessed in my life to truly enjoy each of my different career opportunities, the work and creativity involved in such a dynamic profession, and, most of all, the people, from colleagues to clients to the media. Certainly, there have been challenges, stresses, work crises, and sleepless nights. But each step along the way remains endlessly memorable to me.

What is your career advice?

Do all you can to excel at the position you have and don't worry about next steps — opportunities will come. Work hard. Maintain a constant curiosity and thirst for learning. Be self-aware — understand who you are and the role you play — as you seek to be aware of others. Look to help others. Remember the power of listening. And have fun along the way.

REFERENCE

Coleman, J. (1977). Steve Martin onstage. *New York Magazine*, 10, 49.

13

UNDERSTANDING THE CORPORATE LEGAL DEPARTMENT

Mark Bain[a,b]
[a]upper 90 consulting
[b]Baker McKenzie

"I'm so excited about my meeting with legal today," said no communicator, ever.

Relationships between lawyers and communicators can be rocky. The two occasionally wrangle over what the company should — or should not — do and say.

But their responsibilities and skills make lawyers and communicators essential partners who collaborate on a wide range of matters, including issues and crises that can shape corporate reputation and impact business results.

WHAT LEGAL DOES

Here's a brief look at the legal function and its intersection with communications.

The role and composition of the legal department varies by company type, size, scale, and ownership. But generally, here is what you will find in the legal department of a larger business.

To help their companies grow and prosper, legal teams work to:

• comply with existing laws/regulations;

• advocate for more favorable laws/regulations;

• defend the company in various disputes;

• assist and document corporate transactions;

• ensure proper legal disclosures, internally and externally;

• protect corporate assets, including intellectual property;

• assess and manage business and legal risks.

These departments usually combine legal, regulatory, and government relations disciplines. Communications rarely reports into legal. In 2013, just 6% of communications teams had a solid reporting line and 28% had a dotted reporting line into legal (Swerling et al., 2014).

The Chief Legal Officer and/or General Counsel (GC) leads the department. GCs usually report to, and work closely with, the Chief Executive Officer (CEO). GCs are usually members of the company's senior leadership team (i.e., part of the C-suite).

Legal departments in larger organizations can have dozens of employees. Often, these departments contain a mix of specialists in various practices (e.g., employment law, securities law) as well as legal generalists who work closely with business units and other functions. Paralegals and administrative staff assist in daily work.

WHERE LEGAL AND COMMUNICATIONS INTERSECT

Top legal and communications professionals share important traits. Often, they:

• are passionate about ethics, truth and justice;

• strive to align employee behaviors with corporate values;

• apply a healthy dose of skepticism and caution in their work;

C-suite View

By Craig Meurlin, Former General Counsel, Amway Corp.

Mark has succinctly described the legal function. I want to mention just two legal roles. We protect the company's assets and we help ensure legal compliance. Legal compliance is always cited as a top concern of legal departments.

Often, lawyers do not have a sufficient appreciation of how communications can support these roles. Reputation is perhaps the ultimate corporate asset. I once saw Mark present a global reputation strategy to our executive team. Executives from both operating and staff functions said this could have been the framework for the company's strategic plan.

The biggest opportunity for legal and communications to collaborate, however, is in supporting a corporate culture that champions success and supports legal behavior — where the messaging informs and encourages *actual behaviors* throughout the organization. This requires strong CEO support, but with that support, the combination can be powerful.

Mark used the phrase "envision opportunities" when speaking about communicators while lawyers spot risks. That is a fair comment, but as experienced lawyers know, every word matters. You have not lived until you sit in a courtroom and watch the particular words you wrote in a disclosure document be picked apart by opposing counsel.

- are prepared to confront problems and speak difficult truths to power;
- need visible CEO support to advance their agendas;
- are skilled in using written and spoken words.

Still, there are some notable differences in the way lawyers and communicators think and work:

- Lawyers rely on rules and regulations, while communicators have no such foundation. In providing advice, both exercise judgment based on principles and values, but lawyers can lean on the law to bolster their positions.

- From law school forward, lawyers are trained via the case method to spot risks and mistakes. Good lawyers try to find solutions, but their affinity for problems is one reason why they are often seen as pessimists. Communicators are encouraged to look beyond impediments and envision opportunities.

- Lawyers can potentially bring work to a halt with just one word, "no." Communicators generally don't have that power and must use influence to effect change.

- Lawyers can point to the millions of dollars their work may save the business through transactions completed or revenues preserved with litigation wins. Communicators are still working to prove the financial value of their work.

- Most lawyers prioritize discipline and sweat the details. Many communicators prioritize creativity and don't fret over details.

Finally, communicators should bear in mind that the nature and practice of law is experiencing substantial disruption. There is pressure to control legal expenditures and a push to automate and outsource certain legal work. Concurrently, many more daily company activities are subject to governmental regulations, and some policies are migrating across borders as regulators network and align their regimes.

WORKING WITH LEGAL

Partnering with legal can provide communicators with some of the most intellectually stimulating and professionally rewarding work of their career.

The two play lead roles in just about any business issue or crisis. Their ability to work together and develop effective solutions can help or hurt the business. To illustrate, here is a partial list of the diverse challenges I have tackled alongside my legal colleagues during my career:

• government shutdown of the business;

• corporate restructuring and rebranding;

• corporate reorganization (including large layoffs);

• product recalls;

• high-profile lawsuits with competitors, employees, and others;

• indictment, trial, and jailing of executives;

• office raids by government trade and tax officials;

• gubernatorial campaign of a former chief executive;

• earthquakes, floods, explosions, fires, riots, and coups;

• investigative news stories and attack websites criticizing the business.

In these examples, collaboration between the legal and communications teams greatly benefitted the business. Had we worked independently or failed to align on strategies, the results would have been dramatically different.

There can be tensions, however. Communicators get frustrated when they learn, for the first time, about a major corporate announcement to occur in the next 24–48 hours that lawyers and others have been working on for months. Likewise, in a corporate crisis, communicators want to quickly inform employees and others, but lawyers may oppose any messaging that could potentially be used against the company in future.

At the core of both examples is the need to maintain confidentiality and, by extension, minimize legal and business risk. There

Career Spotlight

By Mark Bain, President, Upper 90 Consulting and Formerly Global Director of Communications, Baker & McKenzie

What was your first job in communications?

I was fortunate to have nine internships while studying advertising and public relations at the University of Utah. These helped me to understand the basics and opened the door for my first full-time job at Burson-Marsteller, a leading global public relations firm where I worked for nearly 16 years.

What is a favorite career memory?

Of many memories, one of my favorites was hearing President Ronald Reagan read a video script I had written for him to assure FIFA, the organizing body for global soccer, that America was willing and ready to host the 1994 World Cup tournament, the largest global sporting event on the planet. It's not every day that a sitting president reads your work word-for-word!

What is your career advice?

It's your career — own it! Become an expert in business, not just communications. Work to ensure that your interpersonal and leadership skills rival your communications skills. Try to be positive, constructive, and encouraging, especially when that's difficult. Most of all, be the change you want to see.

are legal tenets, such as attorney/client privilege, that must be preserved and contracts that strictly limit which executives can know in advance about a merger.

These tensions can be anticipated and avoided, though, if communicators and lawyers both understand the ground rules and review potential scenarios in advance. Beyond this, there is a larger opportunity for lawyers and communicators to drive a deeper discussion with their company's management about risk tolerance — a discussion that could avert problems later.

CONCLUSION

Communicators should develop strong working relationships with their legal colleagues. They don't need to become legal experts, but they should become reasonably fluent in basic legal concepts and processes so they can effectively explain these in messaging. Day-to-day work experience will increase this fluency, as will cross-department training and mentoring.

With this foundation, communicators can become more trusted advisors and indispensable partners to their legal colleagues and others in their organizations.

And when that happens, some communicator, somewhere, will get excited about their upcoming meeting with legal.

REFERENCE

Swerling, J., Thorson, K., Tenderich, B., Yang, A., Li, Z., Gee, E., & Savastano, E. (2014, June). *GAP VIII: Eighth communication and public relations generally accepted practices study (Q4 2013 data)*. Los Angeles, CA: Strategic Communications and Public Relations Center, Annenberg School for Communication and Journalism, University of Southern California.

PART VI

MARKETING, BRAND, AND DATA ANALYTICS

14

DRIVING TO THE RIGHT PLACE: ALIGNING COMMUNICATIONS WITH BUSINESS GOALS AND OBJECTIVES

Joe Jacuzzi[a,b] and Tony Cervone[b]
[a]Chevrolet
[b]General Motors

Before the digital age, a communications professional's role in shaping corporate reputation relied heavily upon instinct, a deep Rolodex and the ability to place — or kill — a story. Next, the digital age gave us reams of data, but without an understanding of the basic concepts of business management (Ragas, Uysal, & Culp, 2015), we lacked the clarity to recognize how that data impacted clients and/or corporate reputations.

Today, the job of a world-class communications professional is not to just serve a client or a company: our job is to understand the data that the ever-changing media landscape provides and forge deeper partnerships with the client and/or departments across the organization so as to drive toward achieving *overall business goals and objectives*.

C-suite View

By Paul Edwards, Vice President, Chevrolet Marketing, General Motors

For the majority of my career, automotive Communications and Marketing worked in somewhat parallel paths. Communications dealt with earned media and Marketing focused on direct customer interfaces. Truthfully, message integration was more the result of luck than planned, fully aligned execution strategies.

That's all changed today at Chevy. Integrated Marketing and Communications is the new norm. We *know* our customers. We share how customers get information. We both understand and work to capitalize on positive customer opinions and overcome negative predispositions. Importantly, we both share the same, very specific, brand reputational goals.

While this relationship may seem entirely logical, the sheer size of the automotive business, the size of the earned media audience, and, candidly, the size of traditional budgets, all led to a complexity of each of our businesses, which allowed us to "go it alone" and appear to be wildly successful. But when we began to work together…to leverage each other's strengths, leverage creative and programmatic systems, and importantly, shared common goals, we have found that our impact has indeed been multiplied exponentially.

And, no matter how big you are, there's always room to do it better, move the needle faster, and improve your relationship with your customer.

THE BOLT EV: ALIGNING COMMUNICATIONS WITH BUSINESS GOALS AND OBJECTIVES

Chevrolet's communications strategy around the launch of the Bolt EV — the world's first "EV for Everyone" — provides a clear example of the level of alignment today's corporate communications professional must have with overall business goals and objectives.

Traditionally, a vehicle is "launched" during the press days of an auto show. While the public days of the show give potential customers the opportunity to see vehicles up close outside of a dealership, the press days are attended by members of what has long been the standard bearer of successful coverage ... the automotive press corps. While this group provided reams of coverage — the essence of "shouting in an echo chamber" by having literally hundreds of stories rolling out from all automakers — the coverage didn't necessarily result in fundamental reputational change. While auto show public days are still very important for consumers to shop and compare vehicles, it had become clear that there was a need for a new way to break through the media clutter.

The core issue at play today is relevancy to wider audiences. Capturing attention of opinion leaders is now less about traditional horsepower and torque, and more about kilowatt-hours and technology. But that was only the first issue. "Where" stories were placed was now becoming more and more important, and simply counting on traditional media who always covered your story was no longer enough.

Wired magazine's 2010 cover story was a harbinger of not only the new media following the industry, but what opinion elites viewed as the new reputation narrative — the electric vehicle race. The headline said it all, "The Age of The Electric Car is Here: How Elon Musk turned Tesla into the car company of the future." The opinion elites saw this as a one-horse race for future domination — there was Tesla Motors and then everyone else.

It's this challenging landscape that Chevrolet found itself in as we prepared to launch the Bolt EV.

The global Chevrolet communications team put a plan in place that incorporated all of Chevrolet's talent, expertise, and data. Aligned with marketing, product development and working with market research, customer profiles, and an understanding of where the customer consumes media, a strategic plan was put in place. This plan was designed to position Chevrolet right in the center of the technology and electrification media discussions — a place Chevrolet was not.

Instead of focusing on the media who were more interested in testing and reviewing Chevrolet vehicles, the communications team — armed with data from colleagues in marketing and advertising — decided to shift the focus away from the automotive press corps (and their 20 million-person traditional automotive enthusiast audience) to the 200 million-person audience of the top digital consumer technology outlets. But we needed to be *relevant* to this broader audience.

AN EV FOR EVERYONE: BRAND STRATEGY AND RESULTS

It all started with a tweet.

In January, 2015 — Mary Barra, Chairman and Chief Executive Officer of General Motors, tweeted a picture of the Bolt EV concept car saying a simple line: "An EV for Everyone." That social ember was the start of what would become a yearlong plan that included working directly with consumers, dealers, media, fans, other stakeholders, and skeptics. The brand was committing itself to democratizing a technology that heretofore had been reserved for the elite (think the Tesla S). Just as the Chevrolet brand was attempting to radically change the discussion around electric vehicles, every traditional idea was analyzed and debated, *not* just by the communications team, but by the entire Chevrolet brand team.

The Chevrolet Bolt EV made its production debut in 2016 at the CES Show in Las Vegas. While the choice of CES in and of itself was a departure from the norm — and part of the strategic shift toward the larger audience presented by consumer technology outlets — the authenticity and relevance was in allowing media to come drive early prototypes of the production car. In other words, the first exposure to the car was not merely a photo opp, but an experience, something Chevrolet needed to do to cement its credibility in this new space.

From that point on, every tactic was designed to build upon that credibility story. For example, when the Environmental Protection Agency (EPA) designated the full range of the Bolt EV in the fall of 2016 — a number that exceeded the expectation set by the original promise from the CEO and the Chevrolet team — Chevrolet didn't just announce the range of 238 miles on a charge, they put media in early cars and let them see how far they could go. This strategy resulted in extensive coverage with both non-traditional and traditional media. More importantly, the credibility gained with this strategy spread into all media coverage, and accelerated the shift in reputation of the brand.

TODAY'S COMMUNICATIONS PROFESSIONAL: A TRUE BUSINESS PARTNER

The Bolt EV is important to Chevrolet and General Motors. It represents a new way of mobility and puts a stake in the ground on technology leadership. Fundamentally understanding the halo potential of this specific vehicle allowed us to make the Chevrolet brand more visible to a massively larger set of potential customers, and helped us maximize the contribution to the overall business objectives of driving net momentum for the brand, which, in turn, has a fundamental role in driving purchase consideration and intention.

The modern communications function — and the modern communications professional — needs to be a strategic partner — as big or as small as what is necessary — to help the client or company to achieve its business goals. To do so, today's professional must understand the business it is representing, not only the

Career Spotlight

By Tony Cervone, Senior Vice President, Global Communications, General Motors

What was your first job in communications?

I was the assistant to editorial services at Chrysler Corporation. In this role, I assisted on speeches/written materials and research/fact support for senior executives at Chrysler, including Lee Iacocca.

What is a favorite memory?

My favorite memory is building one cohesive team from 2003 to 2006 for GM in Europe. When entering the job, we had separate operations by country and by brand. By building on what objectives we all shared, the nature of cross-border communications flow and the strength of the brands collectively, we were able to build one team that worked seamlessly across Western and Eastern Europe.

What is your career advice?

Always stay curious and learn every day. Our profession is changing rapidly, and reputation management is changing. The only way to keep up is to continuously learn. Read about your own industry's challenges and study how others are succeeding or failing. Being a "student" goes well beyond formal classes, books, and exams. It has to be a way of life.

business of "garnering publicity." One must understand which key stakeholders drive the business.

Just as importantly, today's professional needs to understand where these audiences fit in the reputational puzzle, and the process specific stakeholders go through to influence your business... which reputational metrics are important to *them*. It may not be the same for consumers as it is for policy makers, or shareholders or even future employees. But with so much information in the marketplace today, and the ability for audiences to filter information, it is no longer enough to consider good publicity equals a positive impact on reputation, much less an actual impact on your target audiences that will drive a specific behavior. Using new data management techniques, and truly partnering with your key business units, today's communications professional can better target audiences with relevant messaging in places *they choose* to get their most credible information.

REFERENCE

Ragas, M. W., Uysal, N., & Culp, R. (2015). "Business 101" in public relations education: An exploratory survey of senior communication executives. *Public Relations Review*, 41(3), 378–380. doi:10.1016/j.pubrev.2015.02.007

15

PEAS IN A POD: COMMUNICATIONS AND THE CHIEF MARKETING OFFICER

Richard Kylberg
Arrow Electronics

Each time that I walk into a C-level Executive Committee meeting, it feels sort of like an overly serious family reunion.

First off, there's the CEO; our singular embodiment of both mother and father, acting like a circus ringmaster. The Chief Operating Officer (COO) scans the room like an older sister, making sure that everyone knows, and takes, their place. People generally seem to like the kind-hearted little brother with the title of Chief Human Resources Officer (CHRO), but he tends to hide in the back of the room with his overly protective sister, the Chief Legal Officer (CLO). We all cower when our generally grumpy and highly analytical uncle, the Chief Financial Officer (CFO), strolls into the board room to decide if, based on our past behavior, we go to bed with *or without* our supper.

Oh, and then there's me; the wacky, but misunderstood sibling who attracts sidelong glances of curiosity. I am the only functioning twin in the room, and a Siamese twin at that, who's joined at the hip. I am the most senior ranking communications professional in the room, and I am also the highest ranking corporate marketing professional. So, what appears to be two separately confusing functions mash into one individual.

When we really understand the communications and marketing functions and their responsibilities, this oddity ends up making all the sense in the world. At the end of the day, the entire corporate family of senior executives understands that their ultimate success and survival rests on this pair of twins. To survive and to thrive, these functions need to work as one body.

MARKETING AND COMMUNICATIONS: KINDRED SPIRITS

Marketing is one of the least well understood aspects of a corporation because it is sometimes confused with "sales," and, other times, it is viewed as covering only a few aspects of its full portfolio of responsibilities (e.g., it might be viewed as just the "advertising" department). BusinessDictionary.com (2017b) defines marketing to include the "coordination of four elements (called the 4 P's): (1) identification, selection and development of a *product* (or service), (2) determination of its *price*, (3) selection of a distribution channel (or channels) to reach a customer's *place*, and (4) development and implementation of a *promotional* strategy." After that, the rest is implementation.

About communication, BusinessDictionary.com (2017a) states that, "In business, it is a key function of management — an organization cannot operate without communication between levels, departments and employees." Effective communication within an organization is certainly essential, and I can argue that operationally the above marketing definition sounds a lot like at least some of what I do as a communications professional: (1) identify, select, and develop a story or a message, (2) determine its value, (3) select a distribution channel (or channels) to reach an audience's place, and (4) develop and implement a promotional strategy.

Marketing and communications are clearly kindred spirits.

PEAS IN A POD, BUT DIFFERENCES TOO

In many ways, marketing and communications are like two peas in a pod, but there are also differences. The difference between a marketing executive and a communications executive seems to me to rest less in functional differentiation and more in the *types of audiences* or stakeholder groups that each is trying to reach. Marketing tends to focus intently on its current and potential customers, the day-to-day life blood of the company, while communications focuses on all the other constituents who are out there and are not directly measured by revenue generation: employees, media, investors, and other influencers.

In addition to focusing on different audiences, communications and marketing professionals have different feedback loops. It is important to recognize that marketing professionals are constantly under measurement pressure, primarily as it relates to return on investment (ROI), as in: "how much did we just spend and what did we get for it?" This constant need to justify their existence by proving that they are increasing revenue/sales (or related financial metrics), and doing so within the parameters of tightly monitored expenditures, can be limiting and stressful.

At times, marketing professionals will point to their Siamese twin, the communications professional, and say, "We need to measure them, too," but unless the business has clearly defined outcomes or measurement metrics for corporate communications, that can be a fool's errand. As a rule of thumb, because they are on the front lines of selling, marketing executives are generally more highly compensated than communications professionals. This further drives the company's desire to more clearly measure their performance, and might make communications professionals feel a bit better about their relative job security (or not).

GETTING ON THE SAME PAGE

The executive family understands that the shortest professional tenure in the C-suite is frequently Chief Marketing Officers (CMOs). I have heard some senior marketing professionals say that they're only "renting their jobs." So, while these marketing executives may appear to be confident, fancy pants professionals, deep down they are under tremendous scrutiny in their extremely challenging positions. As a result, they will often become best friends with communications professionals who are willing to befriend and support them.

C-suite View

By Mike Long, President, Chairman, and Chief Executive Officer, Arrow Electronics

To more traditional operating executives or other business function leaders, the job of a Chief Communications Officer (CCO) or a Chief Marketing Officer (CMO) can seem confusing and foreign. At the same time, these leaders are so busy overseeing their parts of our business portfolio that they really don't have the time to learn the detail behind the marketing and communication professions (or they sometimes mistakenly think "it's easy").

This means that the most important aspect of the CEO's relationship to his most senior Communications executive is not oversight, but *trust*. Sure, I expect Rich to be the best in the world at this profession, but, even more than that, I need to understand his character and trust him with great authority and responsibility. That's why I brought him into Arrow without corporate experience; I knew him for fifteen years before hiring him, and I knew what I was getting.

If you want to be a successful communicator in a corporation, learn your trade to the best of your ability, but absolutely gain — and keep — the trust of professionals around you. With such trust, like Rich, you will accomplish extraordinary things.

If the marketing and communications function aren't working together every step of the way, the results will be sub-optimal at best. I think of the beer manufacturer with a communications department trying to focus public messaging around sustainable water usage and agricultural awareness around natural hops and barley. Meanwhile, in the marketing department, if a multi-million-dollar ad campaign is about to launch featuring men with mighty muscles dancing about with bikini clad women, an event apparently made possible by copious consumption of this brand of beer ... who's message will get through to the marketplace? Communications departments often can't realistically compete against massive marketing budgets, so it is important for these corporate functions to always be on the same page.

KEY QUALITIES AND CHARACTERISTICS OVERLAP

I would like to add that, in my experience, if an enterprise is concerned about its viability in the long run, the most important characteristic of a marketing or communication professional is probably having the *courage to tell the truth*. Speak truth to power. Marketing and communication campaigns and programs that don't tell the truth might work in the short run, but if a company tricks people, it won't be around long. Those professionals ultimately go to a special place in marketing/communications hell where they are forced to consume their own faulty goods and services for eternity.

The qualities that best suit successful marketing and communications professionals are very similar. The Annenberg School for Communication and Journalism at the University of Southern California reports that the top characteristics for a successful communications professional are empathy, cultural competence, intellectual curiosity, 360 degree thinking, and adaptability to information (Wilson, 2015). When I have looked at lists of traits

Career Spotlight

By Rich Kylberg, Vice President, Corporate Marketing and Communications, Arrow Electronics

What was your first job in communications?

I started as a summer intern at a very small public television station. They didn't know what to do with me, so I asked if I could borrow a camera and editing facilities to do a series of short Public Service Announcements (PSAs). I'm glad that, early in my career, I could do big jobs in a small company rather than small jobs in a big environment.

What is a favorite career memory?

I owned a radio station in New Orleans when Hurricane Katrina hit, and my Chief Operating Officer and I immediately flew into Houston to drive into the closed city. Despite the danger, as communicators, we understood our obligation to the community and went in to try to get the station back on the air to deliver news and prayers for the people. The mayor gave us a service award, but the experience brought home just how important we are in this profession.

What is your career advice?

Just keep striving to do the best work of your life, maybe not every day, but perhaps in looking back quarter after quarter, and asking yourself, "Was that quarter the best I've ever had in my life?" With a cycle of constant improvement, you will never get bored; you are unlikely to lose your job; and you will get old knowing that you did the best that you could.

used to describe successful marketing professionals, it is remarkable to me how much they line up with Communicators.

At the end of the day, marketing and communications professionals can change the world. People tend to believe, repeat, and follow the messages that we send into the world. So ... have the courage to tell the truth. Make good messages. Make kind messages. And, if you don't think this world is quite perfect yet, as a communications professional, it is up to you to grab your marketing colleagues and get out there with your best, most important, and most impactful messages to fix things just the way they really should be in the world!

Welcome to the family.

REFERENCES

BusinessDictionary.com. (2017a). Communication. Retrieved from http://www.businessdictionary.com/definition/communication.html. Accessed on April 25, 2017.

BusinessDictionary.com. (2017b). Marketing. Retrieved from http://www.businessdictionary.com/definition/marketing.html. Accessed on April 25, 2017.

Wilson, E. (2015, June 10). *5 skills employers want that you won't see in a job ad.* Retrieved from http://for.tn/1Mov6HP. Accessed on April 27, 2017.

16

LEARN THE LANGUAGE OF BUSINESS AND KEEP WHAT YOU EARN

B.J. Talley
TE Connectivity

Having previously worked primarily in agencies and at organizations with government customers, joining TE Connectivity, where communications is a part of a broader marketing function, has been a beneficial learning experience. As an almost exclusively business-to-business company, TE's marketing function has a direct and data-driven connection to revenue and profit.

Luckily for me, having a Chief Marketing Officer (CMO) who is a former member of the Arthur W. Page Society, means that strategic communications is an integral part of the marketing strategy. While brand awareness and reputation are critical for TE, for the most part, success is measured in terms of prospects, leads, and the resulting revenue generated.

So what's the connection between marketing and communications, and how do two related — but very different — disciplines interact?

C-suite View

By Amy Summy, Senior Vice President and Chief Marketing Officer, TE Connectivity

I have led marketing teams and advised many organizations over the course of my career. Across those experiences, Marketing had no single design or definition, and, in several cases, Communications was a separate function. At TE Connectivity, Marketing includes Communications. Communications leaders work side-by-side with all leaders to build the company's brand, win and retain customers, and engage employees and stakeholders in TE's purpose and value.

I am particularly passionate about brand. A strong brand drives business value and is the result of significant investment over time. Yet, a brand could lose its value overnight. Marketers tend to focus on brand from a customer perspective. Communications leaders consider additional perspectives — employees, partners, investors, and others. These perspectives improve the results of any brand investment and mitigate risks.

Our world is globally connected and with the rise of digital and social media, I believe organizations are best served to integrate Communications and Marketing. Advertisements and press releases no longer stand alone, a social media post or tweet can have significant consequences, and overcoming a crisis needs strong teamwork and many perspectives. An integrated and strategic Marketing and Communications team will improve results, while ensuring the foundation and strengths of the organization remain intact.

DON'T FEAR THE NUMBERS

The first element of a successful partnership between marketing and strategic communications is to being able to speak a similar language — the language of business. This is a two-way street, of course. Not only do strategic communicators need to understand the marketing strategy and measures of marketing success, we must also be able to relate communications results, as difficult as they can be to measure, into business results.

Marketing metrics — prospects, leads, and sales from leads, for example — are often more tangible and additive than traditional communications and PR metrics. And, whether it is accurate or not, marketers often believe they understand communications and PR metrics better than communicators understand marketing metrics.

So the first step is building your level of awareness and understanding. Participate in marketing meetings, read analyses, and ask questions, all the while thinking about how communications activities and results directly (or indirectly) connect to marketing objectives and deliverables.

Once you have built a level of familiarity, start applying that same data-driven accountability to more and more of your communications efforts. For example, examine share-of-voice among key competitors, instead of just counting impressions for your earned media program. Look at how much traffic a URL placed in a blog post or on an owned social channel drives to a lead-generating marketing campaign site. You will rarely be able to completely quantify the impact of your communications program, but commit to progressively increasing the amount of measureable, impactful business outcomes you aim for.

Over the course of my career, and during my time teaching graduate-level university public relations courses, I heard far too many colleagues and students say that they "went into PR so they didn't have to do math." Well, the days of the smooth-talking spin doctor are largely over: organizations determine success or failure based on tangible business metrics, and strategic communications should do the same.

THE ROLE OF STRATEGIC COMMUNICATIONS

But speaking the same language alone does not necessarily equate to a successful partnership. Strategic communications has plenty to bring to the marketing table — but where exactly does it fit in, and where is it uniquely positioned to create value for the organization?

I am a big fan of sports analogies, so I like to compare the role of strategic communications in marketing as similar to the role of an offensive line in American football. For those unfamiliar with the sport, on any given play, an offensive line player might be fending off an attempt by the opposing team to cause a loss of yardage, or they might be charging downfield to help the ball carrier advance the ball and move the team toward the goal. If you prefer a different brand of football, you can also think of this as similar to the role a midfielder in soccer plays — sometimes defending against an attack and sometimes enabling their own team's advancement by passing the ball.

In both examples, the players must be capable of enabling progress or protecting against loss — and, on many plays, doing both interchangeably. Strategic communications serves much the same role for an organization, and, in particular, for the marketing function.

PROTECTING WHAT YOU'VE GAINED

With the overall role in mind, one of the most impactful roles that strategic communications can play for a marketing function, and for an organization as a whole, is to *protect hard-earned reputational ground*. Organizations spend millions of dollars and thousands of hours of effort to build brand awareness and affinity, but in an increasingly connected and vocal world, a reputational issue or a poorly handled incident can destroy that value almost instantly. And the impact of reputation damage is even more than just the progress lost — it also includes the costs of repairing the damage and the cost of the lost opportunity with stakeholders.

Referring back to the American football analogy, it's the difference between completing a pass to gain 10 yards and being tackled for loss of five yards. The true impact to the team is 15 total yards — the five yards lost and the 10 that could have been gained, as well as the need to waste another play to just get back to where you started. Substitute those yardage numbers with millions of dollars in revenue and you begin to see the need to prevent this sort of thing from happening. You also begin to see how making small, sustained investments in managing reputation can serve as a sort of insurance against these losses of reputational yardage.

Well-known brands like BP, Chipotle, Yahoo!, and United Airlines have all experienced the business impact of poor or non-existent strategic communications in recent years, resulting in combined revenue and market capitalization losses in the billions of dollars. And, while effective strategic communications can't always prevent reputational issues, it can help soften the impact and allow the organization to regain positive momentum more quickly.

When I talk to my marketing colleagues at TE about why communications is important to them, one idea resonates particularly well — a proactive stockpile of reputational capital can help ensure that their efforts and investments will translate into a lasting positive business impact. With that in mind, whether we are launching a brand or product marketing campaign, or announcing an executive transition, we ensure messaging is aligned across a customized array of earned, owned, and paid channels.

BOOSTING MARKETING POWER

In addition to the protective role that strategic communications plays for a marketing function, there is also its ability to serve

as an *accelerant for marketing efforts*. Access to and relationships with an organization's broader community of stakeholders is one of the most valuable ways that communicators
can collaborate with marketers. In my previous sports analogies, think of this role as that of the football offensive line
player running downfield ahead of a ball carrier, which allows
the offense to move the ball even further down the field, or of
the soccer midfielder threading a pass to a barely open forward
near the goal.

Coordinating across channels on something like an upcoming
product launch to gain traffic to a campaign site or to drive direct
customer requests is one of the most obvious and impactful ways
that the two disciplines work together — but that doesn't mean it
is always done most effectively. Collaboration at the very beginning of an effort is key to maximum impact, and ultimately to the
organization achieving the business goal associated with the campaign. A communicator waiting until late in an effort to become
involved or a communicator taking a purely tactical "order-taker"
role severely curtails the strategy and creativity that can be
brought to bear.

The potential for employee communications to enhance marketing efforts can also not be understated. An engaged and informed
group of employee advocates can often be a powerful accelerant for
a brand and its marketing efforts. Southwest Airlines is particularly
adept at this engagement and their employees, who largely shape
the customer experience, have become a differentiator among
airlines.

Alignment between communications and marketing on enterprise
content themes, as well as brand voice and tone, will not only prevent dissonance for stakeholders and maximize the exposure for
specific campaigns, it will help drive greater brand awareness. This
will, ideally, help bring new customers to your brand on their own
volition.

COORDINATION ACROSS CHANNELS

Finally, strategic communicators must help serve as cross-channel coordinators, on behalf of an organization's stakeholders. At TE, like many organizations, marketing staff manage the *paid* and most of the *owned* communication channels, while communications has responsibility for *earned* media.

However, stakeholders rarely delineate between those channels when looking for information, forming an opinion, or conducting business. Regardless of ownership or reporting structure, as the primary connection to all of an organization's stakeholders, it is important for strategic communicators to coordinate across channels and ensure a consistent voice, tone, and experience. When that coordination exists, it builds trust with stakeholders. When it does not, then it erodes trust.

The backlash Pepsi suffered for its 2017 "protest ad," featuring Kendall Jenner seemingly resolving a tense police standoff with a beverage, led to reputational damage, and, presumably, lost revenue for the company. This is a stark example of a decision made around paid media that was almost certainly not effectively vetted by strategic communicators, who should be responsible for knowing *all* of a company's stakeholders well enough to foresee a potential issue like this one.

Stakeholders neither know nor care who controls each channel in a company. They want information, a story, or action — and they will reward or penalize an entire brand based on their experience. When marketing and communications professionals more fully understand what each can bring to the table, organizations are best positioned to build trust, protect reputation, and drive business results.

Career Spotlight

By B.J. Talley, Senior Director of Communications, TE Connectivity

What was your first job in communications?

My internship at Hill & Knowlton during my junior year at the University of North Carolina was when I knew this was the field for me. I worked on a project to advocate for the airport in Gary, Indiana to be a "third airport" serving Chicago — a near-impossible request at the time. Despite the challenge, it was extraordinarily interesting to learn the key issues and stakeholders, and to see the impact of effective communications. I've been hooked ever since.

What is a favorite career memory?

In 2009, I was leading public relations and communications for the division of Maersk that owned the Maersk Alabama, the ship at the center of the piracy incident that inspired the movie "Captain Phillips." When the hijacking happened, I deployed to Mombasa, Kenya to handle media relations. This experience changed the way I approached crisis communications and stakeholder engagement. I didn't make it into the movie (surprise, surprise), but it was a "once-in-a-career" challenge.

What is your career advice?

First of all, say "yes" when opportunities arise to challenge yourself and grow professionally. My second piece of advice is don't specialize in any single "type" of strategic communications, especially in your first few years in the field. The more you know about all channels (earned, owned, and paid), the more effective you will be. Finally, learn the basics of the finances and operations that drive your organization. You don't need an M.B.A., but you need to be able to understand enough to be part of strategic conversations and to know what questions to ask.

PART VII

SOCIAL RESPONSIBILITY AND TRANSPARENCY

17

TRUST, TRUTH, AND TRANSPARENCY: WHY HARD FACTS AND CORPORATE HONESTY MATTER

Matt Peacock
Vodafone Group

It wasn't much of a protest. A couple of young men holding a banner with the words "TAX AVOIDERS" painted in red. They stood silently and self-consciously outside our Annual General Meeting as private investors, many of them elderly, shuffled past them.

"You're wrong," I said to both of them. "Do you know how the tax system works?"

They stared at me as I explained how successive governments had deliberately created incentives to encourage companies to invest that had built up, like soil layers at an archeological dig, into a complex mesh of tax allowances and exemptions. How what they thought were "loopholes" were often no more than political choices made manifest through the tax system.

It started to rain, spattering the banner with long streaks. The accusatory letters grew little pink rivulets. "Whatever," one of them replied. "Nothing any big company says is true. You're *all* liars."

The protester's response was that of hundreds of millions of people. We live in an era of public mistrust. Faith in the large companies that underpin modern economies and societies has greatly diminished over the years. I think the primary reason for this is a widespread belief — constantly reinforced across politics, media, and culture — that large companies routinely and instinctively set out to deceive in response to issues of public concern. While most businesses are run by people with integrity, public skepticism is, sadly, not short of evidence that some are not. But it doesn't have to be like this. There is a gradual revolution underway that, over time, could transform the relationship between corporation and society. At its heart is a commitment to *corporate transparency*.

HARD FACTS, HARD CASH

The tax protests against Vodafone, one of the world's largest telecommunications companies, began in 2010. Media allegations accusing Vodafone of tax avoidance had led to political opprobrium and street protests. When I joined the company shortly after the protests began, it was soon clear that one of the fundamental principles of crisis and issues management was at work. When you're publicly accused of wrongdoing, life gets "binary," fast. Either you've done something wrong, in which case you swiftly apologize, explain what happened, explain how you'll fix it — and the world eventually moves on. Or, you've done nothing wrong, in which case you come out fighting and tell everyone — clearly, loudly and repeatedly — that your critics are mistaken.

Making an accurate distinction between the two strategies — contrition or counter-argument — relies on another fundamental principle of crisis and issues management: it's all about getting

C-suite View

By Serpil Timuray, Chief Commercial Operations and Strategy Officer, Vodafone Group

It is all too easy for a business to turn inward and convince itself that certain truths are self-evident and indisputable while ignoring the evidence to the contrary piling up outside the front door. Executives must be alive to that risk at all times — and none more so than the chief corporate communications officer.

The corporate communications function is most effective when it is expected to challenge internally — asking difficult questions and pushing for credible answers across the business — while simultaneously engaging openly and honestly with external stakeholders. *Presenting the company to the world* is an important aspect of the communicator's role; but so too is the need to *bring the world into the company*, ensuring that managers fully understand and respond to the shifts in public sentiment.

This dual-facing role has assumed even greater importance in the years since the global financial crisis and the subsequent growth of public anxiety about the consequences of globalization. Companies have an urgent need to demonstrate that they have a social purpose as well as commercial objectives — to prove to an increasingly disillusioned public that their core business has a meaningfully positive societal impact.

Effective corporate communications are central to that mission.

---

to the *ground truth*. You need hard facts from within the organization — often directly from the front line — that are uncontaminated by internal spin.

Vodafone's tax affairs are enormously complex — but no more so than the accounting standards and international taxation norms that define them. This was a matter of *transparency*, not malfeasance. What was needed was public proof: unambiguous data and straightforward explanations that would be accessible to non-experts.

In late 2012, we published the first-ever tax transparency report in the global telecoms and technology industry. It contained a comprehensive overview of our tax strategies, set out using simple terminology and with a country-by-country summary of actual cash paid to governments. Nothing was off-limits: every past controversy and allegation was addressed head-on. The level of disclosure was unique at the time and remains so today.

Our tax report was an example of what I call "aggressive transparency" — the strategy of pushing back, hard and through proactive disclosure, whenever the organization is falsely accused. And one year after the first report was published, we discovered that tax wasn't the only area where an aggressive transparency approach would play a critical role in protecting reputation.

SPIES AND SECRET TRUTHS

In 2013, the former National Security Agency (NSA) contractor Edward Snowden claimed that intelligence agencies and telecoms operators (including Vodafone) were colluding illegally to spy on millions of people. His allegations made headlines globally and, as public and customer outrage grew, immediately confronted my company with a very difficult challenge.

With the tax avoidance allegations, it was relatively easy to get to the ground truth. But these were matters of national security. Secrecy and transparency do not go hand in hand: few people know the facts and even fewer can say much about them. We had to focus instead on what we did know. What the law required us to do and how we responded operationally. How our internal rules treated private communications as sacrosanct. How there was sometimes a tension between our own principles and the obligations placed upon us by governments. How we had immediately investigated the Snowden allegations but could find no evidence within our operations to support them.

The result was our law enforcement transparency report. The most comprehensive disclosure of its kind ever published, it explained in detail — and at a country-by-country level — how telecoms operators' legal obligations to assist government agencies and authorities were put into effect at the working level.

Publishing the report involved serious risk. While we avoided revealing information of use to criminals and terrorists, in a number of countries, even the most innocuous discussion of national security matters can lead to arrest. In higher-risk locations, the liberty of some of my colleagues was at stake. Despite this, we all believed we had to go ahead and publish.

CHANGING THE CONVERSATION

Each of the two transparency reports had a significant external effect. The law enforcement transparency report generated headlines in more than 100 countries, prompted parliamentary debates, and was praised by both privacy activists and governments as a strong contribution to a vitally important public debate.

Was the tax report enough for the protestors standing in the rain? No. For some, distrust is too deep-rooted to be healed by any one act of corporate honesty. But it did make the more informed and rational critics realize that their animosity was more usefully directed at a system they didn't like than at a company that had tried — more than any other — to explain how that system worked in practice. The outcome was a different kind of conversation, informed by a shared understanding of the facts.

CHOOSE WISELY

A growing proportion of the public now considers large corporations to be modern demons fully worthy of their role as the villain in countless movies and video games. The perception is a painfully untrue parody: even the small minority of companies that do behave badly invariably do so through cumulative individual acts of stupidity or expediency, not as a result of some great amoral master plan. But it can be difficult — particularly at the outset of your career — to make a clear distinction between businesses that are run by the thoughtful and honest and those that are led by the foolish and spin-addicted. So how do you filter?

First, understand that companies are not *things*, they are *people*; how a company operates is largely shaped by the personalities of its leadership team. Watch and read executive interviews, then ask yourself — would I *like* these people? How would you feel if one of them moved into the apartment next door? If the answer is "probably not," you're unlikely to enjoy the culture of the company they run.

Second, research the most serious and sustained allegations of bad behavior against the company, then look at how it responded. Did it seek to reflect the depth of public concern in making an open and direct disclosure? Or was it silent? The answer will tell you the extent to which the communications function is at liberty to act as the *corporate conscience.*

Throughout, remember this: people gifted with the ability to persuade and influence — *and* who believe strongly in acting with integrity — are a precious talent, sought after at every stage of their communications career. Good companies choose their people wisely — and good people choose their companies wisely.

Career Spotlight

By Matt Peacock, Group Director of Corporate Affairs, Vodafone Group

What was your first job in communications?

I had been on the road as a news correspondent with the BBC and had become weary of journalism after one too many nasty experiences in some tough parts of the world. I moved into a crisis communications consultancy and discovered that being at the center of the action was even more interesting than commentating from the sidelines. From there, I went in-house, with what was then the world's largest internet company, AOL, just as the dot com boom (and bust) happened. I've worked in a variety of different roles, companies, and sectors since then.

What is a favorite career memory?

Whenever I feel my colleagues and I have made a positive difference, whether that's helping to get a multi-billion dollar transaction over the line, or creating innovative safety communications materials for gas and oil installations that help to reduce injuries and fatalities.

What is your career advice?

As one of my CEOs once told me, corporate communicators should have a "license to interfere" if the organization is doing something wrong or misreading signals from the outside world. Use that license wisely and well — and only work for people who understand, value, and respect it.

18

HOW COMMUNICATORS CAN HELP CORPORATIONS MAKE A DIFFERENCE

Stacy Sharpe

Allstate Insurance Company

On September 30, 2016, *The Washington Post* gave its readers a break from the noisy presidential campaign with an opinion editorial from Allstate's Chairman and CEO Tom Wilson called, "How Corporations Can Be a Force for Good." Tom wrote about how successful corporations must do more than focus on the traditional "bottom line" of profits. He challenged the late Nobel Prize-winning economist Milton Friedman's (1970) view that, "There is one and only one social responsibility of business ... to increase its profits so long as it stays within the rules of the game" (p. 125).

The editors questioned us on whether the mention of Friedman would turn off casual readers. We argued for including Friedman. We believe that corporations can — and should — help solve society's problems and be measured in part by the amount of good they do, *not* just how much money they earn. Knowledge of how corporations are measured and where these measures came from are critical considerations as we discuss how businesses are led and evaluated. So Tom pointed out that Friedman's view frames the discussion of the role of business in society. Accordingly, after deliberation, *The Washington Post* editors put the Friedman commentary back in.

COMMUNICATORS AS CHAMPIONS FOR SOCIAL GOOD

One of our most important jobs as communicators is to articulate our company's role and how it creates value for stakeholders. In this case, our message wasn't just about our company; it was about the greater function of corporations in society and how Allstate seeks to lead by example. My team works in concert with Tom, Chief Financial Officer Steve Shebik, the corporate governance team, and senior business leaders to help convey Tom's message that the company's business performance is connected to and foundational for its commitments to other stakeholders.

The idea that corporations can contribute more than profits was included in our Chairman's 2015 annual letter to shareholders. Our CEO's quotes in earnings releases also often reflect Allstate's broader focus on making the lives of our stakeholders better. Some companies leave the details about their societal purpose to their corporate social responsibility (CSR) report. That is changing, however, as more and more firms like ours are examining their roles in society beyond just profits. To build trust in corporations, we must understand how we are measured today and push for broader measures in the future.

COMMUNICATORS AS STORYTELLERS

As communicators, we help people understand the role our businesses play in their lives. While shaping messages for customers, employees and the general public, we are in a comfort zone. But we are sometimes tempted to leave the task of talking to the

C-suite View

By Steve Shebik, Executive Vice President and Chief Financial Officer, Allstate

At Allstate, we expect our leaders to be excellent communicators, and those expectations start at the top. I have worked with CEO Tom Wilson for over two decades and observed the care he puts into his communications with all our constituents, his interaction with the media, and his efforts to make society better. As Allstate's chief financial officer, I try to emulate Tom's example and encourage our executives to consider their words carefully. Such coaching comes naturally to me: my mother was an English teacher.

I expect the same high performance from my communications partners. Just as business leaders need to be excellent communicators, communicators need to have exceptional business acumen. If we're going to work together to make the right strategic decisions for our stakeholders, we all need a deep understanding of what we're trying to do. One example is working on the communications strategy when making an acquisition.

When Allstate acquired SquareTrade, a consumer protection plan provider that distributes through many of America's major retailers, it was critical to communicate the strategic rationale. This acquisition, completed in January 2017, represented an important step for Allstate because it introduced new products and distribution to help protect consumers and expand our customer relationships. Because we were venturing into new territory, we needed to work closely with our communication partners to tell our story. At Allstate, we help customers protect what matters most to them. With that in mind, this product expansion makes perfect sense.

Translating complex business strategy into simple concepts isn't easy, but in the end, stakeholders understood our message. The lesson: Strong communication pays off.

investment community to investor relations and financial communications specialists. We must avoid that temptation: understanding how our businesses make money and impact society is relevant to creating messages for *all our audiences.*

At any corporation, a communications specialist must have a real understanding of and deep appreciation for the business in order to be an effective communicator, influencer, and strategic counselor. Our ability to work in strategic partnership with business leaders is based on deep understanding of our respective businesses and what they mean for employees, customers, investors, and communities.

In addition to strong communications capabilities and learning agility, outstanding communicators not only need to *understand their businesses*, but to *be passionate about them.* Now, before you stop reading in disbelief, know that there *are* people with a passion for insurance.

At Allstate, our shared purpose is to help people. "We are the Good Hands: We help customers realize their hopes and dreams by providing the best products and services to protect them from life's uncertainties and prepare them for the future." So we have a noble purpose. And, yes, our business is fascinating. As former Allstate Chairman Ed Liddy used to say, "Insurance [is] the oxygen of free enterprise" (Boudreau, 2009, p. 671). Think about it. There is very little we do in life without insurance. It gives us the freedom to take risks and the safety net to take care of our loved ones. As communicators, we need to have a real passion for the businesses we support and connect our personal passion to the purpose of the business.

Working closely with senior leaders to tell Allstate's story is the province of our Corporate Communications team. To be effective at the highest levels of a Fortune 100 company such as Allstate, the team needs business acumen, experience and enthusiasm, functional expertise and an ability to see the big picture. No single background or skillset is more important than another: Our team relies on diverse different talents, working together, in a mutually supportive environment.

COMMUNICATORS AS STRATEGIC PARTNERS

To become a strategic advisor, there is no substitute for immersing yourself in the business and learning how it works. But there is more than one way to get there.

Our team includes generalists from PR agencies, as well as experts who worked in the business lines they now serve as communicators. Dr. Jaci Devine, a former professor who joined Allstate in 2015, brought research, teaching, and writing skills honed in academia and put into practice as a business consultant. Similarly, Greg Burns, a longtime journalist who joined Allstate in the same year, put his reporting and writing experience to work from the first day on the job. The broad skills of our team enable us to understand business objectives and align our communication and engagement strategies to meet them.

What can you do to develop your skills? Here are a few suggestions:

- *Learn the business*: Hone your business acumen by rolling up your sleeves and talking with business people. Take graduate-level courses in business and accounting, and seek opportunities to get hands-on experience, whether it's a stretch assignment in your current role, an internship or a fellowship opportunity.

- *Master the basics of effective communications*: Become an expert writer, editor, and presenter. Join professional organizations in the communication field to attend workshops, network and stay on top of the latest trends.

- *Pay attention to the news*: Notice how companies handle stories, good and bad. Read business publications in addition to broader news sources, and follow stories from start to finish. Track your own mini case studies to learn what worked and what did not.

- *Have confidence in yourself and your unique abilities*: When you're a strong communicator who understands the business, you can make a real difference at your company and in society. Don't label yourself in narrow ways. Think of your role and impact in the broadest way possible. Speak up!

Career Spotlight

By Stacy Sharpe, Senior Vice President, Corporate Relations, Allstate Insurance Company

What was your first job in communications?

After working as a management trainee and then in college recruiting at Allstate, my first communications job was for Allstate Indemnity. I managed internal communications and executive positioning. I learned how to support a business through many changes, including an acquisition and a leadership transition. This is when my love for business communications began. It was a great way to learn the business, and achieve rapid personal and professional growth.

What is a favorite memory?

After Hurricane Katrina, when the insurance industry faced negative public perception, Allstate recognized our reputation as a strategic asset. We decided that we needed a research-based way to build and protect it. I led a small team that built our reputation measurement program from the ground up. Today, reputation management is a strategic imperative for our company.

What is your career advice?

Seek out organizations that value communications and be a continuous learner. I have been fortunate to be part of a corporate culture where my colleagues "get it." They understand the importance of effective communications in achieving strong business performance. My job is infinitely better and more enjoyable because I have strong business partners and I am constantly learning and growing.

REFERENCES

Boudreau, J. W. (2009). Allstate's "good hands" approach to talent management: An interview with Ed Liddy and Joan Crockett. In R. Silzer & B. E. Dowell (Eds.), *Strategy-driven talent management: A leadership imperative* (pp. 669–699). San Francisco, CA: Jossey-Bass.

Friedman, M. (1970, September 13). The social responsibility of business is to increase its profits. *The New York Times Magazine*, pp. SM17, SM122–SM125.

19

COMMUNICATIONS FOR SOCIAL GOOD

Andrew Solomon
John D. and Catherine T. MacArthur Foundation

Imagine getting a phone call from out of the blue telling you that you have won $625,000 with absolutely no strings attached.

This dream is a reality for 20–25 highly creative people each year who receive the MacArthur Fellowship, dubbed the "genius grant" by the media. Fellowship recipients work in every field imaginable and have included scientists, historians, poets and novelists, artists and composers, and people focused on public issues. Many work outside of conventional disciplines. Most recipients do not even know they were under consideration when they receive that unexpected phone call from the MacArthur Foundation.

Being present for those life-changing calls is an exciting and emotional part of my job. It reminds me of the transformative potential of philanthropy and the powerful role communications can play in enhancing philanthropy's impact.

Communications is critical to the success and impact of the Fellows Program, both for the Fellows themselves and for the broader public. While Fellows, of course, welcome the financial support provided by the grant, they also benefit from a reputational enhancement that accompanies it. Increased attention from media, those in their field, and the engaged public can lead to more opportunities, more funding, more freedom to follow their own pursuits, and more potential partners for their creative endeavors. A MacArthur survey found that 43 percent of the engaged public are familiar with the program (MacArthur Foundation, 2015).

In addition to supporting the Fellows, MacArthur hopes to inspire the broader public to pursue its own passions and creative pursuits. The diversity of Fellows makes it more likely for a member of the public to see reflected some aspect of his or her own interests, experiences, and identity. Indeed, our survey found that 10 percent of the engaged public (representing nearly 13 million people) say hearing about the Fellows "inspires" them and makes them pause to "think about my work or contribution to society" (MacArthur Foundation, 2015, p. 5).

THE ROLE OF FOUNDATIONS IN SOCIETY

These Fellowships are only five percent of MacArthur's total giving. The Foundation makes grants and impact investments totaling more than $270 million each year to address a range of pressing social challenges, including over-incarceration, global climate change, and nuclear risk. MacArthur supports hundreds of nonprofit organizations working in Chicago, where the foundation was founded and is based, across the United States, and in nearly 50 countries around the world.

In the United States, private foundations like MacArthur, the Bill and Melinda Gates Foundation, and the Rockefeller Foundation help those in need and work to solve social problems. Foundations enjoy considerable flexibility in choosing where to work and what to support. They act independently of any private business and of any government. They are unique institutions — neither businesses

C-suite View

By Julia Stasch, President, John D. and Catherine T. MacArthur Foundation

MacArthur's philanthropy is characterized by big bets that strive toward transformative change in areas of profound concern. This is not a search for quick fixes or easy wins, but an all-in, timely commitment — of talent, resources, time, and reputation — to real change that matters for many, many people. Going all-in requires that we use every means at our disposal to effect genuine and lasting social change. Communications is a powerful and vital tool in this effort.

In some areas of our work, communications is integral to strategy. For example, our *100&Change* competition awards a single $100 million grant to help solve a critical problem of our time. Spreading the word about the competition is essential. Strategic communications helps us to recruit on-target proposals, to draw attention to strong submissions that might attract partners and funding beyond MacArthur's award, to explain how decisions are made, and to inspire the public that solutions to difficult challenges are possible.

We share with our hundreds of grantee partners across the country and around the world a drive for boldness, creativity, and impact. Communications strengthens that effort and tells the story.

selling a product or service nor typical nonprofit organizations, which must raise funds and attract supporters.

For example, John D. MacArthur rose from humble means to become one of the richest men in America. Even after he earned his great wealth in insurance and real estate, MacArthur lived in relative simplicity with his wife Catherine at a Florida hotel he owned, and he often boasted that he did not know his own financial worth. When he died in 1978, he left nearly $1 billion in assets to the Foundation he created. "I made the money; you guys will have to figure out what to do with it," MacArthur told the Foundation's first board.

"WHY DO WE NEED TO COMMUNICATE?"

The day I arrived at MacArthur more than a decade ago to lead the communications team, a new colleague asked me, "Why do we need to communicate? Can't we just make grants and be quiet?" It is a fair, if surprising, question.

MacArthur has three primary reasons to communicate about its work. First, we seek to spotlight the organizations and individuals we support to enhance their reputation, build interest in their work, and encourage other donors to fund them. Nonprofit organizations often view a grant from an established foundation like MacArthur as an endorsement for their work, citing it to other funders, policymakers, and potential partners. To draw attention to grantees and their work, the Foundation may seek press coverage, create videos, support efforts to brief media or policymakers, and use its own website and social media platforms.

Second, we want to educate and inform people about issues that we think matter to building *a more just, verdant, and peaceful world* (our memorable mission statement that you may hear on NPR). We hope doing so will lead to more research, more support from other donors, and to changes in public policy on such issues. For example, reducing over-incarceration in America requires a broader public understanding of the scope of the problem, why it matters, and what is needed to address it. That's why MacArthur seeks media coverage of illuminating research and effective local reforms and awards grants for storytelling by StoryCorps, live events by *The Atlantic*, and in-depth reporting by the Marshall Project.

Finally, we embrace transparency as one of our values. MacArthur is a private institution that serves the public good, so we want to share openly how we are spending our money and why and what we have learned. Also, openness to criticism can make us better and more effective at all we do.

ADVICE FOR THE NONPROFIT COMMUNICATOR

Aspiring and younger communications professionals may think the nonprofit sector holds few career opportunities for them, and they could not be more wrong. The nonprofit community was once much smaller; but it now comprises more than 1.4 million organizations employing 14.4 million people in the United States (McKeever & Gaddy, 2016). Professionals should consider communications career opportunities in this growing sector.

The benefits are clear: challenging work in service of a mission that can be incredibly meaningful. To be fair, the sector tends to underinvest in communications, necessitating an entrepreneurial, can-do attitude to overcome what can be sometimes insufficient resources and staffing.

To be successful as a nonprofit communications professional, it is also important to:

- *Cultivate a broad understanding of the world.* In the nonprofit sector, many issues are intertwined. Housing impacts education and vice versa. Issues of race and class shape significantly the problems afflicting the U.S. justice system. Take the time to learn about the broader context that might impact your work.

- *Recognize that government always matters.* The policies, funding, and rhetoric of government at local, state, and federal levels can enhance or impede the work of every nonprofit. Do not just

Career Spotlight

By Andrew Solomon, Managing Director, Communications, John D. and Catherine T. MacArthur Foundation

What was your first job in communications?

Right after college, I landed a job working on legislation and constituent correspondence for a Massachusetts State Senator. Given the small and busy staff, I was asked to write press releases, newsletters, and a few speeches. That responsibility helped me to realize how much I enjoyed explaining complex public policy to a broad audience. When the Senator lost his bid for re-election just a year later, I learned a quick lesson in the mercurial nature of American politics.

What is a favorite career memory?

When I served as Press Secretary and Director of Public Affairs at the U.S Department of Agriculture during the second Clinton Administration, I traveled frequently with the Secretary. We toured numerous farms, flew in helicopters to view damage from natural disasters, and visited grocery stores in China selling American produce. I was honored to meet some incredible public servants and two personal heroes: President Jimmy Carter and Nelson Mandela. And I was awed by the Secretary's calm and funny reaction when a protester threw a pie at him. "That wasn't a very nutritious meal," he responded without missing a beat.

What is your career advice?

Bring your whole self to all that you do. You are not just a skilled communications professional. You are a person with a range of experiences and relationships, knowledge and ideas, all of which you should draw from in all that you do.

follow the politics but also learn about the policymaking that might matter to your organization.

• *Seek collaboration.* The social challenges that foundations and nonprofits seek to address dwarf the resources that are available. Unlike businesses that compete for resources, our sector values collaboration on shared goals. That collaboration is a source of strength and impact for the sector but also a learning tool for you.

Using strategic communications to effect social change is meaningful work that can make a difference in your community or around the world. And you don't need to receive a surprise phone call from the MacArthur Foundation to find your calling.

REFERENCES

John D. and Catherine T. MacArthur Foundation. (2015, February). *MacArthur fellows program: Summary of 2012–2013 review.* Chicago, IL: John D. and Catherine T. MacArthur Foundation.

McKeever, B., & Gaddy, M. (2016, October 24). The nonprofit workforce: By the numbers. *Nonprofit Quarterly.* Retrieved from https://nonprofitquarterly.org/2016/10/24/nonprofit-workforce-numbers/. Accessed on May 31, 2017.

PART VIII

COMMUNICATION AND
CORPORATE TRANSFORMATIONS

20

BUILDING COMMUNICATIONS' INFLUENCE DURING CORPORATE TRANSFORMATION

Kelly McGinnis
Levi Strauss & Co.

In the corporate world today, businesses are generally doing one of three things — growing, transforming, or maintaining. And let's face it: no one is satisfied with maintenance. So that leaves growth or transformation. A few companies are blessed with hyper growth, but a lot more of us are in organizations fighting hard to turnaround or transform.

There are lots of examples of companies that have made the types of transformations that we all envy. Just think about IBM, Apple, Xerox, or Netflix. But operationalizing change is no small feat. It requires strategic thinking, quality leadership, and the creation of strong partnerships both internally and externally. It means changing how customers, clients, investors, and even a company's own employees think of the business.

As a result, transformation can happen to us as communicators or we can see these as moments of opportunity for corporate communications. Communicators can be leaders — not just enablers — of transformation, driving the change, and understanding that yields business success. That's the lesson that I learned from my last job. And the benefits and opportunities that come with corporate transformation are a big part of the reason I joined Levi's®.

I spent six years working with Dell, and was head of communications for three. Years ago, Dell embarked to transform itself from a low-cost personal computer manufacturer into an end-to-end technology solutions provider.

And today, I'm at Levi Strauss & Co. Like Dell, Levi's® is ubiquitously known. Every day people tell me their Levi's® stories — and *everyone has one*. But here are some things you may not know about Levi's®. We are smaller than you'd expect at just under $5 billion in revenue. For more than two decades, Levi's® pretty much stayed the same size. Five years ago, the Board of Directors brought on a new CEO and challenged him to take the company back to growth mode. And today, we're on track to deliver our fourth year of top and bottom line growth — a level of consistent performance that the company hadn't done in more than 20 years. Despite 163 years of experience, we are still at the beginning of our transformation.

So I guess you could say that I have spent most of the last decade in the trenches of transformation. I appreciate the challenge and — on good days — I thrive on the opportunity. Because as a business leader in transformation,

- I'm required to craft and hone new skills
- I'm forced to build new partnerships
- I'm free to innovate
- I'm able increase my and my department's strategic influence
- And, in the end, I can clearly measure my and my department's impact

I think there are a few things that we can do to ensure that we contribute as transformational leaders versus having transformation happen to us:

- Establish the right team

- Align behind the core narrative and don't waver

- Bring your stakeholder audiences to the table

C-suite View

By Elizabeth Wood, Chief Human Resources Officer, Levi Strauss & Co.

I joined Levi Strauss & Co. as a transformation veteran — having been on the frontlines of multiple apparel companies, including Calvin Klein and Brooks Brothers, that reinvented themselves for the always-changing fashion consumer. In every case, executive leadership thought the silver bullet was people — *too many of the wrong folks and too few of the right ones.*

Often I find myself asking executives — do we need different people or do we need better leadership? Of course, you need the right skills, but most importantly, you need the right vision to guide teams into something new and unknown.

Effective change requires a set of determined and visionary leaders — ones who are allies and partners. At Levi Strauss & Co., part of our approach has been a tight partnership between Human Resources and Communications. Together we have developed a team that serves as the conscience of the organization; leaders who speak the brutal truth, and who make sure that all voices — not just the loudest — are heard.

At Levi Strauss & Co., we have found that the most effective change agents aren't the highest paid people in the room. They are like-minded thought partners who share a vision and want to work together toward a common set of goals. Together, Human Resources and Communications have become a formidable force and, dare I say, unlocked immense value for the company.

ESTABLISH THE RIGHT TEAM

When it comes to tackling transformation, you must first look at your team. It's not enough to simply determine whether you have good people. The question is do you have the *right people* for the job?

Transformation communications isn't for beginners. It takes experience, risk-taking, and conviction. You need folks who have confidence, credibility in the organization, and an eagerness to build influence and make an impact.

So, what kinds of leaders and what key qualities would I choose as my teammates in the transformation trenches? First and foremost, I would say pragmatists. Transformation is messy work with layers and layers of complexity. But as communicators, we have to push hard for clarity and action. In the end, if you are not pragmatic about it, you will never make progress.

Second, leaders who are not only unflappable, but also resilient. In other words, people who are passionate but don't take the challenges and disappointments personally. During a turnaround, your work life will be filled with uncertainty and we just need to bend our knees and ride it through with a focus on consistency — keeping our eye on the ultimate business goal, being the conscience of the organizations, and always delivering for our employees and customers. Every time, no matter what.

Third, optimists. For sure there will be misfires and do-overs in the process, but as leaders we need a team of people willing and able to ask the hard questions while always believing the best is yet to come.

Fourth, it helps, no, actually it's required, that your communicators be courageous. We have to be willing to speak up and speak first. Having a point of view is critical during times of immense uncertainty and imperfect information. And, because we have to push for clarity, it's often required that we make the first effort.

ALIGN BEHIND THE NARRATIVE AND DON'T WAVER

The key to transformation communications is an ability to always work with the "big picture" and long-term business objectives in mind. As a communications team, you must align behind a core narrative and absolutely everything you do should further that agenda.

Doing this well, and doing this successfully, isn't just about repetition. It has to be based on real understanding of the business and how the new company will operate. One of the best pieces of advice I have received is to "trust your Day One key messages." When I look back at most of the big challenges I've tackled, the messages that we started with are usually the ones we're still trying to get across months or years later.

CONVEY OUTSIDE PERSPECTIVES

So much of the work involved in turnarounds is *internally focused*. It takes time, effort, and energy. There are organizations to build, cost savings to find, budgets to negotiate, and myriad competing priorities. But what's so unique — and powerful — about our roles is that we are valued for our connection to *the outside world*.

We are charged with connecting with the stakeholders who matter most and shaping perceptions, whether that's with media, our customers, analysts, or others. Similarly, we are often the convener within our companies. Pulling people together to ensure a consistent message is delivered from every corner of the company, ensuring that our strategies and initiatives will make sense to the outside world. Therefore, it's up to us to be the eyes and ears of the company.

We must always rely on diverse stakeholder inputs and perspectives to inform our recommendations. Without those inputs, it's just opinion. And, just like the credibility that comes with knowing the business, it gives us as communicators the perfect entry point to speak up and go on the record. To be a transformational leader, you have to influence the conversation — and understanding and owning stakeholder perspectives on the business gives the credibility to do so.

KEY TAKEAWAYS

Whether you are in the thick of it now or seeing it come on the horizon, odds are you will spend some time supporting a transformation in your organization. It will be challenging, and hard and time consuming, but it will also be an opportunity —

- An opportunity to shake up your team

- An opportunity to align behind a core narrative

- An opportunity to be nimble and lead, not wait

- An opportunity to "own" data from outside and in

- An opportunity to try something new, to innovate and act differently

The benefits can be exceptionally rewarding and gratifying. You will get to be on the inside of very real and meaningful business lessons. You will increase your business acumen, your ability to counsel and partner with operating executives and to make meaningful contributions to the business. You will be become more influential. If you step up and execute a "company first" strategic communications plan in a time of change within your company, you will strengthen your department's ability to shape decision making inside your company. Finally, you will make some of your most lasting and important work friends. It's inevitable. You will be in a foxhole (whether it's on the other side of activist investors or just a revolving set of C-level executives), and the people you work alongside will be become your trusted friends and advisors for years to come.

Career Spotlight

By Kelly McGinnis, Chief Communications Officer, Levi Strauss & Co.

What was your first job in communications?

I had an internship at King County in Seattle, where I staffed a public–private commission charged with negotiating a labor agreement. I often think of my boss, Pat Steel, with her piercing blue eyes and all of five feet tall. For more than 30 years, she was the resident "fixer." She was always tapped for impossible projects. Her determination — and quirky style — set a high expectation early in my career that strong women get stuff done.

What is a favorite memory?

My best memories are of the people that I've grown up with in this profession. The many amazing and talented professionals who are leading the function at major companies today, but who spent countless hours alongside me sending faxes and working events.

What is your career advice?

Never make career decisions out of fear. Anytime I have made decisions out of fear — fear that I can't recreate the credibility I have built, fear that I won't have the flexibility that I enjoy — I've stayed too long and missed opportunities. But when opportunities terrified me and I still went for it, those are the times that led to step changes in my career.

21

ACCENTUATE THE POSITIVE: THE COMMUNICATOR'S CATALYTIC EFFECT

Jon Harris
Conagra Brands

From a very young age, we learn the power of positive communication. Telling your brother, "It's OK," after he dropped a fly ball — the one that allowed the other team to score the winning run — was more constructive than pointing out that his fielding error lost the baseball game. Better still, your reassuring words were sincere. Maybe, even, the next time you asked your brother to share his candy bar, he happily gave you a piece.

Positive communication can have a similarly powerful effect in business, when it is sincere and when it is *coupled with commensurate actions*. In my role as Chief Communications Officer at Conagra Brands, working closely with Chief Executive Officer Sean Connolly and other members of the executive team, my job is to use communication as a catalyst to transform our company and our culture. Ambitious transformations can be achieved only with the commitment and enthusiasm of every person within the organization, and with the alignment of shareholders, customers, influencers, and media.

Even when the message to be delivered is a challenging one, it is my nature and instinct to *accentuate the positive.*

BUILDING STRONG PERSONAL RELATIONSHIPS

I learned a lot about the power of positive communication at The Sara Lee Corporation, where I had spent a large part of my career prior to joining Conagra. I had come to Sara Lee at the invitation of the late Brenda Barnes, its legendary CEO and a revered leader. I had previously worked with Brenda at Pepsi-Cola North America, where she served as president and CEO, and where her management mantra — "Be tough. Be fair. And always be nice." — was writ large.

At Pepsi, Brenda was a trailblazing executive outside of the office, too. She made headlines in 1997 when she stepped down from her role as the head of the FORTUNE 500 company to care for her young children. Working with Brenda through that experience — of positioning her decision to focus on her family as a positive story, covered by media globally — forged a tremendous professional bond. After she left Pepsi, we stayed in touch as she became both a mentor and friend.

Seven years later, in 2004, Brenda told me she was rejoining the workforce as the CEO of Sara Lee. I was honored when she asked me to head up North American communications, and she cited my positive energy and love of the narrative as key reasons. Working together as an executive team, we greatly improved the reputation and storytelling of Sara Lee, unwittingly preparing the company to go through an unexpected and major transformation.

KEEPING A POSITIVE ATTITUDE IN CHALLENGING TIMES

In May 2010, after several successful years of turning around Sara Lee and at the height of her career, Brenda suffered a hemorrhagic stroke. It was a crisis on many levels: for Brenda personally, her family, for her colleagues and friends at Sara Lee, and for Sara

Lee as a company. CEOs of Brenda's caliber are more than a titular figurehead; they are the heart and soul of the companies they lead. Negative news about key executives can quickly send a company's stock spiraling downward.

Communications professionals pride themselves on being transparent. This situation presented a unique challenge, balancing the *privacy* an individual deserves with the *disclosure* that shareholders and Wall Street expect.

After many hours of meetings with the Board of Directors and a few top executives, we announced that Brenda was taking a leave of absence, thus giving us time to carefully develop, strategize, and announce an executive succession plan. This approach was purposely positive. We gave shareholders the information they needed, while preserving Brenda's privacy and dignity, and bolstered shareholder confidence in Sara Lee's subsequent leadership transition.

We also protected Brenda's privacy by not disclosing her specific medical condition, continuing to balance disclosure and privacy in a series of announcements issued until Brenda chose to retire in August 2010 to focus on her health. I worked with Brenda later as she took the stage at *Fortune* magazine's Most Powerful Women Summit, where she discussed the role her own positive attitude played in her recovery.

COMMUNICATING DURING TIMES OF CHANGE

After Brenda retired, one of our first strategic initiatives was to help unlock shareholder value by splitting Sara Lee into two separate pure-play companies: Douwe Egberts, a global coffee company, and Hillshire Brands, a well-known name that is synonymous with sausage, hot dogs, and other meat products. Sean Connolly then joined as CEO of Hillshire Brands.

C-suite View

By Sean Connolly, President and Chief Executive Officer, Conagra Brands

Jon joined Conagra four months after I took over as CEO. We were in the early stages of disruptive, transformational change. Our communications challenge was to sustain tremendous, rapid change while bringing our people along on the journey, in a supportive way. This required skills, courage, thick skin, and determination. With the Conagra Communications function leading the way, our entire executive team demonstrated all of these things as we navigated through the year.

Throughout the year-long transition, our internal communications emanated optimism and a "can do" spirit, traits that converted many skeptics into believers. The professionalism and consistency of Conagra's new communications approach has led to a seismic shift in our culture; employees now appreciate that we tackle hard change and are excited about our future prospects.

Jon is a strong contributor on the Conagra executive team. He and his colleagues have built a communications function that combines an intuitive understanding of business strategy with the ability to connect with people at all levels. From inspiring our employees, to telling our brand story and realizing Conagra's values as a corporate citizen, communications plays an integral role in achieving our C-suite goals.

Many changes occurred in this corporate transformation, which took place over several years. There were cost-cutting initiatives, job reductions, and significant changes to the business, affecting thousands of employees' lives. Yet, these same employees were critical to the success of the transformation. Their dedication and innovation fueled the company's daily productivity and ongoing success. It was imperative that employees remained engaged and enthusiastic. It was my job to ensure that all team members were fully aligned with our new mission, vision, and values, and knew the role each of them would play in our future success. As a leader, it was critical for me to inject positive energy into the company during this time of tremendous change.

OPEN COMMUNICATION YIELDS POSITIVE RESULTS

During Hillshire's period of extensive restructuring, my team and I developed and led internal communications efforts in which open and positive communication was essential. The focal point of these efforts was a strategic plan of continuous employee communications. Key elements included: town hall meetings, coffee breaks with the CEO and other senior leaders, weekly YouTube-style Sean Connolly videos, regular email updates, monthly key message distribution to our director-and-above leaders, and more. In all communications, employees were encouraged to ask questions and speak their minds, which they did. Sean and other company leaders addressed employee concerns with sincerity and sensitivity.

Throughout the process, we surveyed employees to ensure that they were receiving the necessary information in a timely manner. We received high scores for transparency, openness, honesty, and speed of communications. Productivity, engagement, and innovation remained high.

By having an open dialogue with employees, and clearly explaining their fundamental role in the company's ultimate success, we effectively brought employees "along on the journey." Positive, direct communication between executives and employees played a catalytic role in Hillshire Brands' achieving a successful business outcome: the 2014 sale of the company to Tyson Foods, which won a bidding war for the company after offering Hillshire shareholders nearly a billion dollars over the previous high bid, from Tyson rival Pilgrim's.

In reflecting on my career so far, and distilling 25 years of experience into a few words of advice, I sincerely believe the simplest words ring most true: *Accentuate the positive* by coupling sincere communications with commensurate actions.

Career Spotlight

By Jon Harris, Chief Communications Officer, Conagra Brands

What was your first job in communications?

When I was a student at Rutgers University, I had the outrageous good fortune of landing an internship at WXRK-FM in New York City, home of The Howard Stern Show. It was there that I learned the power of professional relationships; 25 years later, I still keep in touch with many of the people I worked with there.

What is a favorite career memory?

There are so many memories, from meeting Presidents of the United States, to amazing CEOs, to celebrities and athletes; it's impossible to identify one favorite. What I love most is sharing my experiences and learnings with others, to inspire and help them grow as people and professionals.

What is your career advice?

You are your brand! Everything you say or do, whether face to face or on social media, becomes part of your personal brand, which takes time to build but can be tarnished in an instant. Be mindful of what you say and do, and be nice to everyone you interact with. It's that simple.

22

COMMUNICATIONS LEADERSHIP THAT STRONG LEADERS EXPECT

Nick Tzitzon
SAP

On a sunny March day in Northern California, Bill McDermott, chief executive officer (CEO) of business software company SAP, walked into an unremarkable conference room for what would become a remarkable meeting.

McDermott is, in many ways, the dream CEO. Highly energetic and charismatic, he climbed all the way from selling sandwiches as a small business owner to become the first-ever American to lead SAP, Europe's most valuable technology company with 84,000 employees in 190 countries.

Waiting for him that morning were the chief information officers (CIOs) from 30 of the largest companies in the world. They were also some of SAP's largest customers. The discussion began as expected: each attendee introduced her/himself before the group's organizer asked McDermott to deliver some brief opening remarks.

Then things got interesting.

With opening remarks concluded, the CIOs offered the CEO a healthy dose of hard truth. SAP, they said, is a valued business partner. But there are significant challenges. Without a concerted effort by both sides to address those challenges, SAP's strong grasp on supporting the world's largest companies could be at risk.

One CIO framed the discussion: "Bill, everyone in this room wants SAP to succeed. That's why we want you to leave with an unfiltered view of our expectations."

To McDermott's credit, he took the unexpectedly blunt conversation in stride, pledging greater empathy for their concerns and urgent action to address them.

In the weeks that followed, this meeting became a major influence on SAP. Every one of the company's operating divisions had action items and initiatives to deliver on the CEO's commitment.

C-suite View

By Bill McDermott, Chief Executive Officer, SAP

I have always believed that anything worth communicating is almost always *under-communicated*. That's why, as you see in Nick's account, my communications team is at my side every single day in everything I do as CEO.

To every aspiring communications leader, I would remind you that trust is the ultimate human currency. To earn the trust of your leaders, prove to them that you understand the fundamentals of the business. Give them candid advice, based heavily on a true "outside-in" perspective.

If you deliver, they will welcome you into the inner circle and never want you to leave.

INTEGRATED COMMUNICATIONS LEADERSHIP

In case you haven't realized it yet, this scenario is entirely about smart, integrated communications leadership. Let's dissect it.

Who is the audience? Every business has customers. The customer audience is often the most significant priority audience for a communications team. Don't forget to prioritize! If you try to be all things to all people, you'll end up as nothing to anyone. In this case, getting the CEO in front of this group was a communications-led initiative. Unfiltered feedback to executives is critical to helping them lead the business. It also helps shape messages that are relevant and directly connected to keeping and growing a happy customer base.

What is the primary message? Communications leadership can be like coaching a sports team: everyone else is the expert and thinks their playbook is better. In this example, it was clear that the CEO had decided on an over-arching message to guide SAP's reaction. "Empathy to Action" became that rallying cry. Enter communications: to firmly establish this message, define its parameters and organize the disparate efforts across the company that belonged in this unified story. A strong and substantive integrated plan was needed to get the company's executives and spokespersons on the same page. Such a plan took constant alignment with product- and customer-facing teams so that all of the latest content was included from the ground up. Communications leadership is about filling vacuums and scaling the management prerogatives of the CEO.

How do you disrupt the crowded information environment? Every audience — internal and external — is overwhelmed by *too much content* from *too many sources*. In a situation like this, communications leadership is about taking a business-critical message and making it consumable for the priority audiences. This takes a combination of tactics, some new and others time tested. Put your leaders out front fast — a major CEO keynote address to set the stage and establish the program. Align your surrogate speakers and train them ferociously to be effective messengers. Be creative — where can videos, infographics, and social media shake things up and keep the message simple?

How do you use a message to change a culture? It is tempting to measure communications with metrics like share of voice, impressions, or views. The reality is that communications is fundamental to running, growing and changing a business and its culture. Here the CEO understood instantly that this one meeting could ignite a new clarity of focus across the company. He turned to his communications leaders because he knew that no team could do more to help him scale this moment into a *change mandate*. Instead of a one-off meeting, he wanted additional candid meetings with knowledgeable stakeholders, including customers and industry analysts. He wanted colleagues to feel empowered to elevate feedback they were receiving about opportunities for improvement. In the case of every expectation, it was the responsibility of the communications function to take the lead in achieving those outcomes.

How do you maintain momentum? From that first meeting, empathy to action has consumed SAP. The company was recently validated on *The Empathy Index* as one of the ten most empathetic companies in the world (Parmar, 2016). Industry analysts have openly acknowledged the significance of SAP's "Empathy to Action" campaign. Employees are hungrier to admit and confront challenges. In a follow-up meeting of the CIO group, there was strong consensus that SAP had responded with vigor. Success in this case is ultimately a race without a finish line, but the progress is palpable.

BUSINESS ACUMEN: KEY TO THE OFFICE OF THE CEO

Every 21st century CEO is, by default, a chief communications officer (CCO). Like for Bill McDermott in our example, the expectations on top leaders in business to communicate effectively are higher than ever — from shareholders who want transparency, from customers who want empathy, from colleagues who want clarity. But this is only half the story! If CEOs are now expected to be skilled communicators, we in the communications profession are expected to be business strategists. It's very much a two-way street.

Understanding this reality is the first step to helping your executives and colleagues across the organization build a truly engaging and effective approach. This adds value on a day-to-day basis and, especially, in situations that were never anticipated. Be knowledgeable, be credible, and be fast.

How do communicators cross-over into business strategists? This is not rocket science. Make changes to your daily routine. For example, instead of reading only what the clipping service sends, boost your daily intake of the business press. Instead of looking past your points of confusion about the company's balance sheet, call up a colleague in finance or investor relations and dedicate an hour for a tutorial. Also, read your annual report. Yes, all of it. This will help challenge you to go one or two levels beyond the soundbites and blog posts that communicators are normally responsible for creating. If doing so causes you trouble, it is a safe bet that your lack of depth will also show itself in front of senior executives. If you dedicate yourself to knowing more about the business, you are already taking a major step closer to the boardroom.

What is the secret to success building trust with senior executives? First, see above. The one thing most leaders in business have in common is that they can sense uncertainty from a mile away. If you aren't prepared, you won't be successful. Beyond that, remember that bringing value to any discussion is about bringing a valuable point of view. Communicators "own" audiences — it's the one asset we have in our portfolio that we are expected to know better than anyone else. So walk confidently

Career Spotlight

By Nick Tzitzon, Executive Vice President, Marketing and Communications, SAP

What was your first job in communications?

I was the Communications Director for John Guerin, mayoral candidate in my hometown. In those pre-social media days, our entire day on the campaign trail depended on the delivery of the local newspaper. It was our one shot to get the message right, otherwise we'd have to endure a full day's worth of grumbling at the grocery store and the coffee shops. I still remember the beat reporter's name — Jason Grosky. Our fate was almost totally in his hands. John won big. Anonymous sources close to the campaign credited the communications strategy (wink).

What is a favorite career memory?

On a road trip with Health and Human Services Secretary Tommy Thompson, he asked me to find him a place to watch the Green Bay Packers on Monday Night Football (he was Governor of Wisconsin for 14 years). Every bar was filled with fans watching the baseball playoffs. Secretary Thompson said, "you're a communications person — figure out what to say so they will change the channel!"

What is your career advice?

No task that matters to the team is beneath you. When I was a young intern in Massachusetts state politics, I interviewed to work for a powerful former prosecutor, Chris Supple. When Chris called my former supervisor, the feedback was, "See that flagpole out on the lawn? That kid would climb to the top and clean it if you asked him to." This approach has served me well to this day.

with the knowledge that you bring an "outside-in" perspective. Share it in a constructive way so that your leaders believe you are opening new doors for them.

This, together with a deep understanding of the business, are your keys to the C-suite.

REFERENCE

Parmar, B. (2016, December 20). The most empathetic companies, 2016. *Harvard Business Review*.

PART IX

SUMMING UP

23

OBSERVATIONS AND CONCLUSIONS FROM "MASTERS OF BUSINESS"

Matthew W. Ragas and Ron Culp
DePaul University

Two-lane roads work best when drivers respect both lanes. The same can be said for the relationship between strategic communications professionals, the C-suite and business unit leaders. Over the past decade, the strategic communication profession has been largely successful in educating business people — from the corner office to newly minted MBAs — about the value of effective strategic communications and investing in the communications function (e.g., Arthur W. Page Society, 2007, 2013a, 2013b, 2016, 2017a, 2017b; Daniels, 2015; Laskin, 2011; Neill, 2015; Ragas & Culp, 2014a).

But this is a two-way street.

If business people are to entrust strategic communications professionals with greater leadership roles and responsibilities within the enterprise, then, in turn, communicators must be increasingly well versed in the "business of business" (see APCO Worldwide, 2016; Claussen, 2008; Duhé, 2013; Feldman, 2016; Ragas, 2016; Ragas & Culp, 2013, 2014b, 2015; Ragas, Uysal, & Culp, 2015; Roush, 2006; Sahel, 2017; Spangler, 2014; Turk, 1989; Wright, 1995).

Writing in his chapter Nick Tzitzon the head of marketing and communications at SAP, the giant global software company, describes this two-way relationship between the skills and competencies of C-suite leaders and communicators in this way: "If CEOs are now expected to be skilled communicators, we in the communications profession are expected to be business strategists. It's very much a *two-way street.*"

A famous phrase from Stephen Covey, cited by Peter Marino of MillerCoors in his chapter, is perhaps most instructive of *why* business acumen is so critical to unlocking the full potential and value of strategic communications on behalf of organizations, their stakeholders, and society. According to Covey (2004): "Seek first to understand, then to be understood" (p. 247).

Whether a communications professional is tasked with serving as a convener, integrator, translator, brand storyteller, or reputational steward, a communicator should first fully *understand* the business challenge, problem, issue, or opportunity. Without such important context, the chances of being *understood*, whether by colleagues across the enterprise or external stakeholders — and providing counsel that resonates and is followed — is greatly diminished.

This final chapter attempts to summarize and synthesize some of the key themes that the more than 20 CCO contributors and their C-suite counterparts expertly provided in their chapters. As such, this chapter starts by discussing two key observations: the role of communications as courageous counsel and corporate conscience, and its heightened focus on employee engagement and corporate culture. The chapter then summarizes the characteristics and capabilities CCOs indicate they want on their communications teams, and their advice for younger professionals on navigating their communications careers. Next, actionable advice from CCOs on "learning the language of business" is briefly reviewed. Finally, the chapter concludes with closing thoughts from the editors on the future of the strategic communications profession.

COURAGEOUS COUNSEL AND CORPORATE CONSCIENCE

CCO contributors and their C-suite counterparts emphasize throughout their chapters the central role of the communications function — due in part to its broad view across the enterprise and beyond — in providing "courageous counsel" to senior leadership, including the CEO. Several contributors explicitly call communicators the "corporate conscience" of an organization. Such observations echo prior academic and applied research (e.g., Berger & Meng, 2014; Bowen, 2008, 2009; Harrison & Mühlberg, 2015; Marshall, Fowler, & Olson, 2015a, 2015b).

For example, Rich Kylberg of Arrow Electronics argues that perhaps the most important characteristic of a communications professional is "having the courage to tell the truth" and "speak truth to power." Similarly, Kelly McGinnis of Levi Strauss & Co. believes communicators should serve as "the conscience of the organization; leaders who speak the brutal truth, and who make sure that all voices — not just the loudest — are heard." Finally, Matt Peacock of Vodafone Group believes the communications function is most effective "when it is expected to challenge internally — asking difficult questions and pushing for credible answers across the business — while simultaneously engaging openly and honestly with external stakeholders."

So why does the communication function have the mandate in some organizations to provide courageous counsel and serve as the corporate conscience? In part, these communications teams seem to be headed by leaders who are trusted and respected by the C-suite, and in which senior executives recognize and value what Serpil Timuray, chief commercial operations and strategy officer of Vodafone Group, calls the "dual facing role" of communications. According to Timuray, communications professionals help *present the company to the outside world*, while *bringing the world inside to the company*, thereby helping the C-suite and senior leaders to more fully understand stakeholder sentiment and opinions.

SAP CEO Bill McDermott explains further: "To earn the trust of your leaders, prove to them that you understand the fundamentals of the business. Give them candid advice, based heavily on a true 'outside-in' perspective." According to multiple C-suite leader sidebar remarks, communication professionals that demonstrate their stakeholder insights are grounded in a *deep understanding of the business* are more likely to have their counsel sought out — and followed. For example, Steve Shebik, chief financial officer of Allstate, makes the following case: "Just as business leaders need to be excellent communicators, communicators need to have exceptional business acumen. If we're going to work together to make the right strategic decisions for our stakeholders, we all need a deep understanding of what we're trying to do."

HUMAN CAPITAL, EMPLOYEE ENGAGEMENT, AND CORPORATE CULTURE

In addition to providing courageous counsel and serving as corporate conscience, CCOs emphasized how human capital and company cultures are critical sources of competitive advantage. Effective external communications remains important, but excellent internal communications has moved front and center on the CCO agenda (Men & Bowen, 2017). Predictably, chapters in which CCOs wrote about their relationship with the human resources function and corporate transformations focused on employee engagement and internal stakeholders. But, even in chapters in which the focus was on working with functions such as investor relations (Carole Casto), marketing (B.J. Talley), strategy and innovation (Linda Rutherford) and legal (Mark Bain), these CCO contributors discussed more effective employee engagement and understanding as desired outcomes of these functional relationships.

For example, Linda Rutherford of Southwest Airlines explains in her chapter taking on the challenge to "communicate the amoeba" — the company's new corporate strategy. Rutherford and her team's challenge was to make this new strategy "real" for Southwest's employees. This required a high level of business acumen from her team to translate this multi-year strategy roadmap into five major pillars that were relatable to Southwest's thousands of employees.

"It's about more than just putting a comma in the right place; it's about understanding the business and how it makes money to turn around and communicate something to a group of employees that will help them be educated, inspired, and engaged," says Rutherford. "Understanding leads to engagement."

Corey duBrowa, now the CCO of Salesforce and previously the top communicator for Starbucks, tells a similar story in his chapter, which is appropriately titled, "Mastering Business Means First Understanding Your People." duBrowa credits Starbucks' "people-first point of view" with helping to "build and preserve the culture that is so fundamental to Starbucks business success." duBrowa says that Starbucks strives to make decisions on corporate strategy and how best to grow its business "through the lens of [its] partners," which is how Starbucks refers to its employees. "We already know that our partners are our most important asset: the frontline "face" of our brand, engaging daily with millions of customers in thousands of stores around the world," explains duBrowa.

One of the seven Page Principles of the Arthur W. Page Society (2017b), a professional association for senior public relations and corporate communications leaders, is: "realize an enterprise's true character is expressed by its people" (para. 8). This principle goes on to state that, "the strongest opinions — good or bad — about an enterprise are shaped by the words and deeds of an increasingly diverse workforce." While all stakeholder groups — from customers to investors — receive attention in these pages, it is undeniable that the CCO contributors to this book show a collective commitment to this principle, and view excellent employee engagement and company cultures as particularly critical to driving sustained business success.

WHO DO CCOs WANT ON THEIR TEAMS?

CCO contributors seek an array of knowledge, skills, and capabilities in their team members, but some consistent themes emerged from their chapters. These senior leaders generally seek professionals with impeccable communication chops (e.g., writing, editing, presenting, and related technical skills), strategic thinking and proactive problem solving, a commitment to continuous learning amidst a fast-changing field, and team members who demonstrate high integrity and don't hesitate to share their (well informed) point of view. Stacy Sharpe of Allstate implores communication professionals to "have confidence in yourself and your unique abilities" and "speak up!" while Peter Marino of MillerCoors says "don't be afraid to debate colleagues to make the outcome better" and "never, ever be bashful!"

CCOs generally indicate that professionals need to invest in boosting their business acumen so they can work more effectively across departments, functions and stakeholders in helping an organization define and achieve its business purpose, strategies, goals, and objectives. As Joe Jacuzzi and Tony Cervone of General Motors explain: "The modern communications function — and the modern communications professional — need to be a strategic partner — as big or as small as what is necessary — to help the client or company achieve its business goals."

While hard skills are important, CCOs consistently highlight in their chapters the importance of specific soft skills and character traits in the professionals they want on their teams. This includes professionals being passionate about what they do, optimistic in the face of challenges, and having a positive mindset. For example, Kelly McGinnis of Levi Strauss & Co. acknowledges that "for sure there will be misfires and do-overs" but "we need a team of people willing and able to ask the hard questions while always believing the best is yet to come."

In short, not just technical skills, but the attitude, demeanor, and interpersonal qualities of professionals are generally valued by these CCO contributors. For example, Jeffrey A. Winton of Astellas credits his farm upbringing with understanding that "humility, gratitude, hard work, and perseverance are critical in the business setting, especially working with the C-suite." He advises communicators to "check [their] ego at the door." Winton says that, throughout his career, he has tried to surround himself with positive, sincere, humble, genuine, and fun colleagues.

THE JOURNEY TO BECOMING A LEADER

An analysis of the backgrounds of the book's CCO contributors suggests there is *no one path* to becoming a senior communications leader. Many contributors recommend that aspiring and younger communications professionals enjoy the journey and be open to new paths. CCOs come from quite a range of backgrounds and experiences. First jobs in communications for the senior leaders in this book included everything from working in radio (Clarkson Hine, Jon Harris) and journalism (Matt Peacock, Linda Rutherford) to politics (Chuck Greener, Clarkson Hine, Matt Peacock, Andy Solomon), government offices/agencies (Carole Casto, Kelly McGinnis), sports information (Gary Sheffer) and health care (Kathryn Beiser). Anne C. Toulouse started out as a civilian writer-editor for a division at Patrick Air Force Base. Other contributors got their start in agencies (Mark Bain, Corey duBrowa, B.J. Talley, Jeffery A. Winton) and corporate positions

(Tony Cervone, Stacy Sharpe). Multiple contributors were entrepreneurs with their own businesses, including Peter Marino founding his own agency (Dig Communications, now OLSON Engage) and Rich Kylberg owning a radio station group.

Multiple CCOs advise readers to focus less on career advancement, and more on continual learning and being open to new career experiences. For example, Kathryn Beiser, previously a senior communications leader with Edelman, Hilton Worldwide and Discover Financial Services, advises: "Pursue *learning* first — which can involve some detours — and *advancement* second. Each experience makes you a stronger, more substantive professional. If I had pursued a linear path, I might never have enjoyed such a satisfying career."

Multiple CCOs recommend that professionals continually pursue new roles and responsibilities that make them uncomfortable, and help broaden their experiences and skills. According to Kelly McGinnis of Levi Strauss & Co., "when career opportunities terrified me and I still went for it, those are the times that led to step changes in my career." Tony Cervone of General Motors offers a similar thought, recommending that younger professionals "always stay curious and learn every day." He suggests "being a 'student' goes well beyond formal classes, books, and exams. It has to be a way of life." Rich Kylberg of Arrow Electronics recommends professionals commit to a "cycle of constant improvement."

Several CCO contributors also emphasize the importance of a professional's personal brand and reputation to one's career advancement, as well as professionals "taking ownership" of their own careers. Jon Harris of Conagra Brands states simply: "you are your brand!" He goes on to advise: "Everything you say or do, whether face to face or on social media, becomes part of your personal brand, which takes time to build but can be tarnished in an instant. Be mindful of what you say and do, and be nice to everyone you interact with." Gary Sheffer, the former long-time

CCO for General Electric, advises professionals to "own [their] career" and think about one's strengths and weaknesses, then "seek training, advice, and experience that can address them." He recommends that professionals "put [their] hand up for 'stretch assignments.'" Former CCO Mark Bain has a similar message as Harris and Sheffer: "It's your career, own it!"

ACTIONABLE ADVICE ON "LEARNING THE LANGUAGE OF BUSINESS"

CCO contributors provide in their chapters no shortage of actionable advice and ideas for improving one's business acumen at all career stages. Further, CCOs were frank in noting that, just as one does not learn to speak fluent Spanish or French after one high school class, it takes time, effort, and perseverance to become fluent in business disciplines such as finance, accounting, management, and marketing. Peter Marino of MillerCoors remarks in his chapter that his first few weeks of his MBA program "felt like [he] was learning a foreign language in a new country."

Many contributors recommend that professionals immerse themselves in business and industry news sources as a way to learn the language of business and of particular industries. Linda Rutherford of Southwest Airlines provides in her chapter an excellent set of additional recommendations for younger communications professionals to "get smart" on business:

- Read an organization's quarterly earnings reports and financial statements.

- Seek out younger professionals in other departments to do an informal exchange of knowledge about your departments and functions.

- Seek out mentors with subject matter expertise to help grasp the more complex topics in your industry and better understand (and explain) them.

- Take business classes and read business books to enlighten you on different business terms and industry opportunities, challenges, and trends.

Rutherford's recommendations pair very well with a set of recommendations from Clarkson Hine of Beam Suntory's chapter on how professionals can get more "Street smart" (i.e., learn more about how Wall Street and financial-oriented stakeholders think and operate):

- Review presentations from investor conferences of relevant public companies, including your own company, if it is publicly traded, and peers/competitors

- Access and read reports by Wall Street investment analysts who cover relevant public companies in your industry and sector, including your own if it is public

- If you're in a position to request a company's strategic plan and any internal competitive analysis, request it, and study these materials.

- Finally, watch the business news channel CNBC to gain expose to a range of different voices, such as CEOs, analysts, investment fund managers and business reporters, to accelerate learning the language of Wall Street and business.

On a related note, communication professionals of *all* experience levels can benefit from building and maintaining strong relationships across the enterprise, and strong external professional networks. Such relationships provide mentors, advisors, and subject matter experts that can serve as valuable tutors and sounding boards on the nuances of businesses and careers.

Carole Casto of Cummins Inc. emphasizes this point about networking in her chapter:

> *Your peers will be some of your biggest allies along your career journey. Be sure to keep in touch with college classmates, colleagues, and anyone else who interests you professionally. These contacts can be counted on at almost any step of the way throughout your career by providing knowledge, answering questions, and helping you keep a pulse on happenings in your area of expertise.*

LOOKING AHEAD

The outlook for the strategic communications profession and related communications field is bright. Stakeholder demands for greater corporate transparency and accountability (DiStaso & Bortree, 2012; Hardeck & Hertl, 2014; Rawlins, 2009), the increasing need for businesses to earn and keep the trust of *all* stakeholders (Uysal, 2014; Uysal & Tsetsura, 2015), and C-suites generally recognizing the value of corporate reputations and other intangible assets (Byrum, 2013; Laskin, 2016; Ragas & Culp, 2014a) are all positives. Projections are for strategic communications and related professions, such as marketing, to grow about as fast or faster than the overall U.S. economy in the years ahead (U.S. Bureau of Labor Statistics, 2017).

But continued growth in communications jobs does not necessarily equal increased influence by the profession within corporations (Neill, 2015) and, in turn, shaping corporate purpose and character. Corporate boardrooms, executives and investors are demanding greater corporate efficiencies, including better integration among departments and corporate functions. In the years ahead, more strategic communications and public relations teams, including chief communications officers (CCOs), could conceivably become part of marketing departments — unless they make compelling cases otherwise (Daniels, 2015; Haran & Sheffer, 2015; USC Annenberg Center for Public Relations, 2017). In a time of corporate transformations, it is critical that communications leaders earn and keep their roles as trusted advisors to the C-suite and other executives (Arthur W. Page Society, 2017a; Ragas & Culp, 2014a).

Whether working in human resources, technology, legal, accounting, or communications, a high level of business acumen is a differentiator for those who seek leadership roles, since functional expertise is a given (see, e.g., Duhé, 2013; Ragas, et al., 2015; Spangler, 2014). A greater focus on the integration of business and communication skills as part of talent development in the years ahead is likely to pay big dividends for the profession as a whole (Bain & Jain, 2015; Bain & Penning, 2017; Commission on Public Relations Education, 2012, 2015; Ragas, 2016). To revisit a phrase that was introduced in the preface, to maximize the future impact of the profession within the enterprise and beyond: *strategic communicators need to be business people with an expertise in communication.*

For those who understand these rules of the road, this two-way street has never looked better.

REFERENCES

APCO Worldwide (2016, November). *Chief corporate communicator survey*. Chicago, IL: APCO Worldwide.

Arthur W. Page Society. (2007). *The authentic enterprise: An Arthur W. Page Society report*. New York, NY: Arthur W. Page Society.

Arthur W. Page Society. (2013a). *Corporate character: How leading companies are defining, activating and aligning values.* New York, NY: Arthur W. Page Society.

Arthur W. Page Society. (2013b). *The CEO view: The impact of communications on corporate character in a 24×7 digital world.* New York, NY: Arthur W. Page Society.

Arthur W. Page Society. (2016). *The new CCO: Transforming enterprises in a changing world.* New York, NY: Arthur W. Page Society.

Arthur W. Page Society. (2017a). *The CEO view: Communications at the center of the enterprise.* Retrieved from http://bit.ly/2q4t2UI. Accessed on May 4, 2017.

Arthur W. Page Society. (2017b). The Page principles. *AWPageSociety.com.* Retrieved from http://www.awpagesociety.com/site/the-page-principles. Accessed on May 1, 2017.

Bain, M., & Jain, R. (2015, October). *Higher value through higher performance: Findings from quantitative research on talent development and management in communication.* Grand Rapids, MI: Upper 90 consulting.

Bain, M., & Penning, T. (2017, March). *Understanding high performance in corporate communications functions today: Key insights from in-depth interviews with Chief Communications Officers.* Grand Rapids, MI: Upper 90 consulting.

Berger, B. K., & Meng, J. (Eds.). (2014). Public relations leaders as sensemakers: A global study of leadership in public relations and communication management. New York, NY: Routledge.

Bowen, S. A. (2008). A state of neglect: Public relations as "corporate conscience" or ethics counsel. *Journal of Public Relations Research*, 20(3), 271–296.

Bowen, S. A. (2009). What communication professionals tell us regarding dominant coalition access and gaining membership. *Journal of Applied Communication Research*, 37(4), 418–443. doi:1080/00909880903233184

Byrum, K. (2013). *PRSA MBA program: Bridging the gap between strategic communications education and master of business administration (MBA) curriculum*. New York, NY: Public Relations Society of America.

Claussen, D. (2008). On the business and economics education of public relation students. *Journalism & Mass Communication Educator*, 63(3), 191–194.

Commission on Public Relations Education. (2012, October). *Standards for a master's degree in public relations: Educating for complexity*. New York, NY: The Commission on Public Relations Education.

Commission on Public Relations Education. (2015, May). *Summary report: Commission on Public Relations Education's (CPRE) industry-educator summit on public relations education*. New York, NY: The Commission on Public Relations Education.

Covey, S. R. (2004). *The 7 habits of highly effective people: Powerful lessons in personal change*. New York, NY: Simon & Schuster.

Daniels, C. (2015, April 10). How the CCO role is changing – It's complicated. *PR Week*. Retrieved from http://bit.ly/1yjqReE. Accessed on May 1, 2017.

DiStaso, M. W., & Bortree, D. S. (2012). Multi-method analysis of transparency in social media practices: Survey, interviews and content analysis. *Public Relations Review*, 38(3), 511–514. doi:10.1016/j.pubrev.2012.01.003

Duhé, S. (2013, December 12). Teaching business as a second language. *Institute for Public Relations*. Retrieved from http://bit.ly/1cGKcsw. Accessed on April 21, 2017.

Feldman, B. (2016, November 28). Dear comms exec: Basic business skills are still required. *PR Week*. Retrieved from http://bit.ly/2ovUmWt. Accessed on April 20, 2017.

Haran, L., & Sheffer, G. (2015, March 24). Is the chief communications officer position going the way of the dodo? *PR Week*. Retrieved from http://bit.ly/1OLpY3z. Accessed on May 1, 2017.

Hardeck, I., & Hertl, R. (2014). Consumer reactions to corporate tax strategies: Effects on corporate reputation and purchasing behavior. *Journal of Business Ethics, 123*(2), 309–326. doi:10.1007/s10551-013-1843-7.

Harrison, E. B., & Mühlberg, J. (2015). *Leadership communication: How leaders communicate and how communicators lead in today's global enterprise.* New York, NY: Business Expert Press.

Laskin, A. V. (2011). How investor relations contributes to the corporate bottom line. *Journal of Public Relations Research, 23*(3), 302–324. doi:10.1080/1062726X.2011.582206

Laskin, A. V. (2016). Nonfinancial information in investor communications. *International Journal of Business Communication, 53*(4), 375–397. doi:10.1177/2329488414525458

Marshall, R., Fowler, B., & Olson, N. (2015a). *The chief communications officer: Survey and finding among the Fortune 500.* Los Angeles, CA: The Korn Ferry Institute.

Marshall, R., Fowler, B., & Olson, N. (2015b). *Trusted counsel: CEOs expand C-suite mandate for best-in-class corporate affairs officers — and especially for the strategic advice they provide.* Los Angeles, CA: The Korn Ferry Institute.

Men, R. M., & Bowen, S. A. (2017). *Excellence in internal communication management.* New York, NY: Business Expert Press.

Neill, M. S. (2015). Beyond the C-suite: Corporate communications' power and influence. *Journal of Communication Management, 19*(2), 118–132. doi:10.1108/JCOM-06-2013-0046

Ragas, M. (2016). Public relations means business: Addressing the need for greater business acumen. *Journal of Integrated Marketing Communications, 17,* 34.

Ragas, M., & Culp, R. (2013, Spring). Taking care of business: How PR pros and academics can build a stronger profession. *The Public Relations Strategist,* 15–16.

Ragas, M., & Culp, R. (2014b, December, 22). Public relations and business acumen: Closing the gap. *Institute for Public Relations.* Retrieved from http://bit.ly/16MJ33P. Accessed on May 1, 2017.

Ragas, M., & Culp, R. (2015, May 1). Business week: Five ways to build greater business acumen. *Public Relations Tactics,* p. 17.

Ragas, M. W., & Culp, R. (2014a). Business essentials for strategic communicators: Creating shared value for the organization and its stakeholders. New York, NY: Palgrave Macmillan.

Ragas, M. W., Uysal, N., & Culp, R. (2015). "Business 101" in public relations education: An exploratory survey of senior communication executives. *Public Relations Review, 41*(3), 378–380. doi:10.1016/j.pubrev.2015.02.007

Rawlins, B. L. (2009). Give the emperor a mirror: Toward developing a stakeholder measurement of organizational transparency. *Journal of Public Relations Research, 21*(1), 71–99. doi:10.1080/10627260802153421

Roush, C. (2006). The need for more business education in mass communication schools. *Journalism & Mass Communication Educator, 61*(2), 195–204.

Sahel, J. (2017, February 14). The inner circle. *Briefings* (Korn Ferry Institute). Retrieved from http://www.kornferry.com/institute/the-inner-circle. Accessed on April 20, 2017.

Spangler, J. (2014, June 2). Valued communicators understand the business. *Institute for Public Relations.* Retrieved from http://bit.ly/1xiYB8n. Accessed on June 6, 2017.

Turk, J. V. (1989). Management skills need to be taught in public relations. *Public Relations Review, 15*(1), 38–52.

U.S. Bureau of Labor Statistics. (2017). *Occupational outlook handbook, 2016–2017 edition.* Washington, DC: Office of Occupational Statistics and Employment Projections.

USC Annenberg Center for Public Relations. (2017, March). *2017 global communications report.* Los Angeles, CA: USC Annenberg School for Communication and Journalism.

Uysal, N. (2014). The expanded role of investor relations: Socially responsible investing, shareholder activism, and organizational legitimacy. *International Journal of Strategic Communication, 8*(3), 215–230. doi:10.1080/1553118X.2014.905478

Uysal, N., & Tsetsura, K. (2015). Corporate governance on stakeholder issues: Shareholder activism as a guiding force. *Journal of Public Affairs, 15*(2), 210–219. doi:10.1002/pa.1529

Wright, D. K. (1995). The role of corporate public relations executives in the future of employee communications. *Public Relations Review, 21*(3), 181–198. doi:10.1016/0363-8111(95)90020-9

ABOUT THE AUTHORS

Mark Bain is president of upper 90 consulting, a practice that helps leaders and their teams adapt, grow, and excel. He helps departments in large corporations deliver greater business value through functional assessments, organizational design, professional development, executive coaching, and other tools. Previously, Mark headed internal and external communications worldwide at Baker McKenzie, a leading global law firm. Before that, he held a similar position with Amway Corp., a top global direct selling company. At Amway, he reported to the company's General Counsel for several years. Mark began his career with Burson-Marsteller, a leading public relations firm. He worked in the firm's New York, Los Angeles, Hong Kong, and Tokyo offices during his time there. In partnership with universities, upper 90 consulting conducts research into talent management, professional development, and high-performing teams in corporate communications. Mark is a member of the Arthur W. Page Society.

Kathryn Beiser has worked across a broad range of industries during her career both as a chief communication officer and as an agency executive. Most recently, Kathryn was Global Chair of the Corporate Practice at Edelman, where she was responsible for building the firm's portfolio, counseling clients, leading the development of the Edelman Trust Barometer, and strengthening the firm's capabilities. Prior to joining Edelman, Kathryn served as executive vice president of corporate communications for Hilton Worldwide, as well as head of corporate communications for Discover Financial Services. She also spent several years working at some of the world's leading public relations firms, including

Burson-Marsteller, Golin, and Hill & Knowlton. Kathryn is a Trustee of the Arthur W. Page Society and a former trustee of the Institute for Public Relations. She holds a bachelor's degree in political science from Northwestern University and a master's degree from the Medill School of Journalism at Northwestern.

Roger Bolton is the president of the Arthur W. Page Society, the premier professional association for senior corporate communications executives. He is a trustee and a past chairman of the Page Society. Previously, he served as senior vice president of communications at Aetna, with responsibility for all internal and external communications, advertising, brand management, and corporate public involvement. Before Aetna, Bolton was IBM's director of corporate media relations and director of communications for the IBM server and software groups. Prior to his business career, Bolton served as assistant secretary of the Treasury for public affairs under President George H. W. Bush, special assistant to President Reagan in the White House, and assistant U.S. trade representative for public affairs under President Reagan. Bolton is a recipient of the U.S. Treasury Distinguished Service Award and a Lifetime Achievement Award as a Thought Leader in Trustworthy Business Behavior from Trust Across the World.

Carole Casto serves as the vice president of marketing and communications at Cummins Inc. where she oversees marketing communications and corporate communications. Prior to her communications role, Carole held leadership positions in both Corporate Responsibility and Quality. Before joining Cummins, Carole worked for the State of Indiana, serving as the Chief Operating Officer for the Family and Social Services Administration and Department of Environmental Management. She is a recipient of the *Indianapolis Business Journal's* Forty Under 40 designation and was selected as one of the top 100 women alumnae from Marquette University. In 2011, she was a recipient of the Boston College Corporate Citizenship Film

Festival Award for her work on a video depicting innovative power generation in India. Carole and her husband, Bill Barnhorst, reside in Indianapolis, Indiana with their son, Leo.

Tony Cervone was named senior vice president, global communications, General Motors Company in May 2014. As GM's top communications executive, he is responsible for the company's overall global communications strategy, including the GM Foundation and corporate giving activities. Prior to his current position, Cervone served as executive vice president of Group Communications for Volkswagen Group of America. He also was senior vice president and chief communications officer for United Airlines. Cervone was previously at GM from 1999 to 2009 in various executive roles. He began his career at Chrysler Group and DaimlerChrysler AG. Cervone earned a bachelor's degree from Central Michigan University where he majored in Journalism. He is a member of the Arthur Page Society, the Public Relations Society of America, and The Seminar. He is a board member of The LAGRANT Foundation.

Ron Culp is a veteran public relations executive whose career includes senior roles in government, corporations, agencies, and academia. Before joining DePaul University's College of Communication as professional director of the public relations and advertising graduate program, he was managing director of Ketchum Chicago, where he also headed the global agency's North American corporate practice. Prior to his agency career, he headed public relations and government affairs at Sears following senior corporate communications roles at Sara Lee Corporation, Pitney Bowes, and Eli Lilly. Upon graduation from Indiana State University, he became a newspaper reporter before moving into government roles in both Indiana and New York. As professional in residence at DePaul, Ron teaches courses about Chicago corporations, agency management, and leadership. In addition to co-editing *Mastering Business for Strategic Communicators*, Ron writes the popular PR career blog, Culpwrit. He is co-author with Matthew W. Ragas, Ph.D. of *Business Essentials for Strategic Communicators: Creating Shared Value for the Organization and Its Stakeholders* (Palgrave Macmillan, 2014). Ron is active in several industry and civic organizations and is the recipient of numerous awards, including PRSA's prestigious Gold Anvil, both the Hall of Fame and Distinguished Service Awards from the Arthur W. Page Society, and is listed in Crain's Who's Who in Chicago Business.

Corey duBrowa is executive vice president and chief communications officer for Salesforce, the global leader in CRM. Previously, Corey was senior vice president, Global Communications for Starbucks, leading the development and execution of communications strategies to enhance and protect the company's brand and corporate image. Prior to joining Starbucks in 2010, he spent a decade as President of the Americas and Business Development at WE Worldwide, consulting with clients ranging from Microsoft to T-Mobile to Toshiba. Prior, he led employee communication efforts and urban marketing strategy for the U.S. region at Nike. He holds a B.A. in journalism from the University of Oregon, and served as President of the University of Oregon Alumni Association for two years and its board of directors for seven, and President of the School of Journalism and Communications Advisory Council from 2012 to 2014. He was served on the Arthur W. Page Society Board of Trustees and Board of Advisors for the USC Annenberg Center on Communication Leadership & Policy since 2015.

Paul Gerrard has three decades of public relations and marketing communications experience in corporate and consulting environments, driving growth, and creating long-term value by protecting and enhancing corporate brands and reputations. He is the vice president of strategic communications at the Blue Cross Blue Shield Association (BCBSA), a national federation of 36 independent, community-based and locally operated Blue Cross and Blue

Shield (BCBS) companies. In this role, Paul serves as an executive officer and chief communications officer, responsible for developing and managing BCBSA's communication functions, integrated public relations strategy and national corporate social responsibility efforts. He also provides crisis communications, media relations, and public affairs counsel to BCBS company executives nationwide. He joined BCBSA from Humana, Inc. where he was director of corporate affairs, and, prior to that, he was president and a partner in Public Relations Network, a leading agency in the Mid-West. A native of the United Kingdom, Gerrard began his career in European public relations, including serving as public affairs manager for Bass PLC. Paul earned a bachelor's degree from the University of Kent. He is a PRSA Silver Anvil recipient, a member of the Arthur W. Page Society and has served on multiple boards throughout his career.

Chuck Greener is senior vice president, global corporate affairs and communications for Walgreens Boots Alliance. Prior to joining Walgreens in 2010 and continuing at Walgreens Boots Alliance, Greener held several senior positions for Fannie Mae in Washington, DC, from 2001 to 2009, ultimately as chief communications and marketing officer and chief of staff to the CEO and Chairman of the Board. From 1995 to 2001, Greener led Porter/Novelli's office in Washington, DC, and headed the firm's public affairs practice. Greener has been involved in politics and government for more than 30 years, including serving in the Office of Legislative Affairs in the Reagan White House, as well as a Congressional Chief of Staff, and heading communications for the Republican National Committee under chairman Haley Barbour from 1993 to 1995. He has also run a number of election campaigns for the U.S. House and Senate as well as Governor in the states of Ohio and New Jersey. Greener received his B.A. in history and political science from Valparaiso University.

Jon Harris is the chief communications officer at Conagra Brands, where he reports directly to the chief executive officer. He is privileged to work with a CEO who understands that communication is paramount to the successful transformation of the company and its culture. As a kid who grew up in Wayne, NJ, it's been a thrill for Jon to work with presidents, celebrities, and many amazing colleagues throughout his 25-year career in communications. After starting on the public relations agency side, he has had had the honor of protecting and enhancing world-class brands at Pepsi, Bally Total Fitness, Sara Lee and Hillshire Brands. Jon has done everything from launching soft drinks, to handling crisis communications, to engaging employees globally, to helping ensure the success of multi-billion dollar corporate transactions. In all of these roles, he has worked closely with multiple teams to ensure clear, cohesive communications with employees, shareholders, customers, influencers, and media.

Clarkson Hine is an enterprise-wide senior executive with experience in building, promoting, and protecting the reputation of public and private companies, consumer brands, and business and political leaders. He also is experienced in crisis communications and advocating for global public policy interests in a highly regulated industry. Clarkson is currently senior vice president − corporate communications & public affairs at Beam Suntory, the world's third largest premium spirits company. He is responsible for the company's strategic communications programs, including external communications, internal communications, and corporate social responsibility, and leads the company's global public affairs/government relations function. Before entering business in 1998, Clarkson served in senior communications positions on the Senate leadership, presidential campaign, and post-election staffs of Senator Bob Dole, including three years as press secretary during Dole's high-profile tenure as both Minority and Majority Leader of the United States Senate.

Joe Jacuzzi is executive director, Global Chevrolet Communications. Prior to this appointment, Jacuzzi had served as vice president and chief communications officer for Audi of America, responsible for overseeing internal and external communications of the company, including employees, dealers, customers, the media, and other constituencies. Joe has had public relations and communications roles in car companies including Audi, Ford, GM, Nissan, and Mitsubishi. He also helped build PepsiCo's beverage-communications team as its vice president of beverage communications. Jacuzzi also has launched automotive aftermarket-technology startups. Joe has held a variety of communications assignments both domestically and globally for GM, including leading U.S. Chevrolet communications, product and brand communications for GM Europe, for GM in the United Kingdom and for GM in Latin America, Africa, and the Middle East. Jacuzzi has a lifetime enthusiasm for performance cars and racing. He grew up watching and racing at various tracks in Northern and Southern California.

Richard Kylberg serves as the senior executive overseeing corporate marketing and communications at Arrow Electronics, an 80-year-old, Fortune 150 corporation with offices in 58 countries. In five years, he developed a stunning brand message and architecture, uniting this highly fragmented company around the world, and increasing its brand value to approximately $2 billion. For the past four years, Arrow has ranked as Fortune's "Most Admired Company" in its industry. Prior to joining Arrow, Rich spent 20 entrepreneurial years owning radio stations across the United States. He is a five-time Ironman finisher, and was a qualifying member of Team USA for long course triathlon. Rich holds a Bachelor of Arts degree from Stanford University, and a Master of Business Administration from Harvard Business School.

Peter Marino has more than 20 years of experience in public relations, government affairs, and strategic consulting. As the chief public affairs and communications officer for MillerCoors, Marino is a member of the Senior Leadership Team, the Strategy Committee, the Operating Committee, and reports directly to the CEO. Marino is also the president of Tenth and Blake Beer Company, the company's craft and import division. He is the founder of Dig Communications, which was known for a terrific company culture, outstanding creativity, client service, and results. Marino sold Dig to Olson in November 2010 and left in 2012 to join longtime client MillerCoors. Earlier in his career, he held positions with Miller Brewing Company, Boston Consulting Group, Cramer-Krasselt, and Ketchum. Marino holds an MBA from The Anderson School at UCLA and a B.A. in journalism from the University of Wisconsin at Madison. Marino is a member of the Arthur W. Page Society and The Seminar.

Kelly McGinnis, as chief communications officer of Levi Strauss & Co., is responsible for managing the global Corporate Affairs function at the 160-year-old apparel company. In this capacity, she oversees corporate media relations, executive, internal and stakeholder communications, government affairs, social responsibility, and community affairs. Kelly reports to CEO Chip Bergh. Previously, Kelly was the vice president of global communications at Dell. Prior to joining Dell, she served as general manager of Fleishman-Hillard's San Francisco office after working with the firm in various capacities in St. Louis and San Antonio. Earlier in her career, Kelly led corporate communications for drugstore.com. Kelly is a two-time Silver Anvil award recipient. She holds a master's degree in public administration from the University of Washington and a bachelor's degree from Miami University in Oxford, Ohio.

Matt Peacock is group director of corporate affairs at Vodafone where he leads the company's communications and sustainable business strategy across more than 40 countries. He was previously the group communications director with the global oil and gas exploration and production company BG Group and has held communications director roles with the UK communications regulator Ofcom, mobile network operator 3, and the global internet service provider, AOL. He is a former radio correspondent with BBC News and has reported on assignments across Europe, the Middle East, Asia, and the United States.

Matthew W. Ragas is an associate professor in the College of Communication at DePaul University where he teaches courses at the intersection of strategic communication, business, and society. He has served as academic director of DePaul's award-winning public relations and advertising graduate program. In addition to co-editing *Mastering Business for Strategic Communicators*, Matt is the author or co-author of three other books including *Business Essentials for Strategic Communicators: Creating Shared Value for the Organization and Its Stakeholders* (Palgrave Macmillan, 2014), co-authored with Ron Culp. An award-winning teacher and researcher, his scholarship and commentary have been published in many of the top academic journals and trade publications in the field. Prior to academia, Matt worked in investment research and publishing, financial communications and venture capital. A founding member of the Arthur W. Page Society's Page Up organization, he is honored to have served as faculty adviser on multiple student case studies that have won the Jack Koten Page Principles Case Study Award. He holds a Ph.D. in mass communication with a focus on corporate communication from the University of Florida, and master's and bachelor's degrees in business administration from the University of Central Florida.

Angela Roberts is chief marketing and communications officer for the American Veterinary Medical Association. She was previously managing director of strategic communications at the Blue Cross Blue Shield Association. In this role, Angela led multiple teams including internal communications, HR communications, digital communications, and a group dedicated to communicating to the

36 independent BCBS companies. She has 20 years of experience in strategic marketing and corporate communications with experience across industries including healthcare, engineering, technology, higher education, finance, and publishing. She has led communications activities at Cancer Treatment Centers of America (CTCA), Johns Hopkins University, Agora Publishing, Legg Mason, and local non-profit organizations. Her expertise is in strategic communications, marketing, branding, writing and editing, market research, and digital communications. Along with a Bachelor of Arts degree from University of Maryland, Baltimore County, Angela earned a Master of Arts degree from Johns Hopkins University. She also earned a certificate in strategic marketing from Northwestern University's Kellogg School of Management.

Linda Rutherford is senior vice president and chief communications officer for the nation's largest domestic airline, Southwest Airlines Co., based in Dallas, Texas. Her leadership includes guiding the efforts of Media Relations, Employee Communications, Emergency Response and Business Continuity, Strategic Public Relations, Social Business, Charitable Giving and Community Relations, Visual Communication, Employee Engagement & Travel, and Community Affairs, and Grassroots. Prior to joining Southwest, she was a reporter for the *Dallas Times Herald* newspaper and has an extensive newspaper and magazine reporting background. She has a Bachelor's degree in journalism from Texas Tech University. Among her civic and professional activities are board positions with the Texas Tech Alumni Association, Lewisville ISD Education Foundation, and Institute for Public Relations, as well as membership in the Arthur W. Page Society. She also has been involved in chamber boards, and state and national nonprofits. She and her husband, Michael, have two children, Matthew and Allison.

Stacy Sharpe is senior vice president, corporate relations at Allstate Insurance Company. In her role, Stacy helps tell Allstate's story of transformation and growth by leading internal and external communications for Allstate's CEO, chief financial officer and the major businesses in the Allstate family. Amplifying the voice of Allstate has been a theme for Stacy in her 21 years with the company. In addition to Corporate Relations, she has been a leader in business operations, federal affairs, and human resources. She serves on the Board of Directors of the Chicago Urban League and on the Chicago Advisory Board of Facing History and Ourselves. She was named in The Hill publication's 2011 list of Top Corporate Lobbyists and she is a 2007 Fellow of Leadership Greater Chicago. Stacy holds a Bachelor of Arts in English Literature from the University of Virginia and an MBA from the University of Illinois at Chicago.

Gary Sheffer is a respected global leader in communications strategy, crisis management, and culture change. He served as Chief Communications Officer for most of his 16 years with General Electric and is now a senior corporate strategist for global public relations firm Weber Shandwick. At GE, Sheffer served as GE's chief global reputation officer, developing protocols for crisis, risk assessment, and tactical execution. Working with the CEO, he developed strategic communication and cultural platforms, including branding and reputation initiatives. Sheffer began his career as a journalist, winning awards for his newspaper reporting and writing. He moved on to public information, serving as a press aide to two New York governors. Sheffer is a past chairman and trustee of the Arthur W. Page Society, the premiere global organization for senior corporate communicators. He serves on the boards of the Institute for Public Relations (IPR) and the Arthur W. Page Center at the Penn State College of Communications. He received IPR's Jack Felton Gold Medal for Lifetime Achievement, and is a member of the PR News and *PR Week* halls of fame.

Andrew Solomon is managing director, communications, at the John D. and Catherine T. MacArthur Foundation, one of the nation's largest private philanthropies. He directs the Foundation's strategic efforts to use communications to help effect social change. Before joining MacArthur in 2005, Solomon served as Director of Communications & Strategy for Harvard University's Institute of Politics. Previously, he was Director of Public Affairs for the U.S. Conference of Mayors, as well as Director of Public Affairs & Press Secretary for the U.S. Department of Agriculture during the second Clinton Administration. Solomon has also worked as Chief of Staff and Press/Legislative Aide in the Massachusetts State Senate, editor of a budget travel guide, college radio station news director, and an intern at least four times. He holds a Bachelor's degree from Harvard University and a Master's in Public Policy from Harvard's John F. Kennedy School of Government.

B.J. Talley is a senior strategic communications practitioner and educator with experience in leading strategic communications for government agencies, international private firms, and publicly traded companies. He currently serves as the senior director of communications for TE Connectivity, a $12 billion global technology company that designs and manufactures key components for transportation, industrial applications, medical technology, energy, data communications, and the home. He is responsible for all of the company's internal, external, and crisis communications, as well as for safeguarding corporate reputation in the 150 countries where TE does business. B.J. previously taught graduate-level strategic communications courses at American University in Washington, DC; and, prior to that, served in a variety of communications roles at ITT Corporation, A. P. Moller-Maersk, Booz Allen Hamilton, and the U.S. Navy.

Anne C. Toulouse is vice president of Global Brand Management and Advertising for Boeing, the world's largest aerospace company and leading manufacturer of commercial jetliners and defense, space and security systems. She is responsible for the company's global brand-building programs, including digital and advertising strategy, brand sponsorships, the Boeing Stores, and corporate identity. In 2016, she had the good fortune to lead the huge, multi-channel Boeing centennial initiative. In 1989, Toulouse joined McDonnell Douglas as manager of Media Relations for space and defense programs in Huntington Beach, California. Later she served as director of Communications at the same site. Boeing and McDonnell Douglas merged in 1997; Toulouse moved to Chicago in 1999 to take the position of vice president of Corporate Identity and Advertising, and then vice president of Business Operations for Communications. She served as vice president of Employee Communications from January 2008 through July 2014. She began her career in 1980 as a civilian writer-editor with the U.S. Air Force. Following that assignment, she worked in media relations and served as a spokesperson for two dozen space launches and missile tests, later moving into the position of chief of Community Relations. Toulouse holds a Bachelor of Science degree from Florida State University.

Nick Tzitzon is executive vice president of marketing and communications for SAP. Reporting to SAP CEO Bill McDermott, Nick oversees SAP's 2000 marketers and communications professionals. He has nearly two decades of communications experience in the public and private sectors. Before joining SAP, he supported a range of clients including the U.S. Small Business Administration, the University of Illinois and Kronos, Inc. During his career in politics and public service, he worked for former Massachusetts Governors Paul Cellucci and Mitt Romney. At the national level, he helped count hanging chads during the infamous 2000 Florida recount and was a high-ranking appointee at the U.S. Departments of Justice and Health and Human Services. A highly overrated recreational tennis player, Nick once hosted a weekend talk radio show on WLS-AM in Chicago. He is an active supporter of the Alzheimer's Association and the We Are Family Foundation.

Jeffrey A. Winton is senior vice president, corporate affairs for Astellas Pharma. In this role, Winton is responsible for corporate brand and reputation management, where he leads a multi-faceted team of communications, corporate social responsibility and events, government affairs, policy and advocacy professionals. Winton is a member of the Astellas Americas Management Committee and also serves as the executive sponsor of Astellas' People Living with Disabilities employee resource group. Before joining Astellas in 2013, Winton served as the vice president and head of global communications at other leading pharmaceutical and agricultural companies, including Eli Lilly and Company, Schering-Plough, and Pharmacia. Winton earned a Bachelor of Science in life sciences from Cornell University in Ithaca, New York. He serves on the Cornell University CALS Advisory Council. A Board member of the Public Relations Society of America Health Academy, Winton was recognized as the first recipient of the PRSA Health Academy Excellence in Public Relations Award. He is a recipient of The Plank Center Milestones in Mentoring Award and has also been named PRSA Chicago Chapter Public Relations Professional of the Year and IABC-NJ Communicator of the Year. Winton is a member of The Seminar and the Arthur W. Page Society, two leading professional associations for senior public relations and corporate communications executives.

RESOURCES ON BUSINESS ACUMEN

JOURNAL ARTICLES ON BUSINESS ACUMEN AND COMMUNICATIONS EDUCATION

Claussen, D. (2008). On the business and economics education of public relation students. *Journalism & Mass Communication Educator, 63*(3), 191–194.

DiStaso, M. W., Stacks, D. W., & Botan, C. H. (2009). State of public relations education in the United States: 2006 report on a national survey of executives and academics. *Public Relations Review, 35*(3), 254–269. doi:10.1016/j.pubrev.2009.03.006

Dolphin, R. R., & Fan, D. (2000). Is corporate communications a strategic function? *Management Decision, 38*(2), 99–106.

Laskin, A. V. (2011). How investor relations contributes to the corporate bottom line. *Journal of Public Relations Research, 23*(3), 302–324. doi:10.1080/1062726X.2011.582206

Laskin, A. V., & Fussell Sisco, H. (2015). Math apprehension of public relations students: An experiment. *Teaching Public Relations, 91*, 1–4.

Marron, M. B. (2014). Graduate degrees in journalism and the MBA. *Journalism & Mass Communication Educator, 69*(3), 3–4. doi:10.1177/1077695814523933

Neill, M. S., & Schauster, E. (2015). Gaps in advertising and public relations education: Perspectives of agency leaders. *Journal of Advertising Education, 19*(2), 5–17.

Pardue, M. J. (2014). Most business editors find journalism graduates still unprepared. *Journalism & Mass Communication Educator*, 69(1), 49–60. doi:10.1177/1077695813506989

Ragas, M. W., Uysal, N., & Culp, R. (2015). "Business 101" in public relations education: An exploratory survey of senior communication executives. *Public Relations Review*, 41(3), 378–380. doi:10.1016/j.pubrev.2015.02.007

Roush, C. (2006). The need for more business education in mass communication schools. *Journalism & Mass Communication Educator*, 61(2), 195–204.

Turk, J. V. (1989). Management skills need to be taught in public relations. *Public Relations Review*, 15(1), 38–52.

Wright, D. K. (1995). The role of corporate public relations executives in the future of employee communications. *Public Relations Review*, 21(3), 181–198. doi:10.1016/0363-8111(95)90020-9

Wright, D. K. (2011). History and development of public relations education in North America: A critical analysis. *Journal of Communication Management*, 15(3), 236–255. doi:10.1108/13632541111151005

BOOKS RELATED TO STRATEGIC COMMUNICATIONS AND BUSINESS ACUMEN

Akerlof, G. A., & Shiller, R. J. (2009). *Animal spirits: How human psychology drives the economy, and why it matters for global capitalism*. Princeton, NJ: Princeton University Press.

Appleby, J. (2010). *The relentless revolution: A history of capitalism*. New York, NY: Norton.

Berger, B. K., & Meng, J. (Eds.). (2014). *Public relations leaders as sensemakers: A global study of leadership in public relations and communication management.* New York, NY: Routledge.

Bronn, P. S., Romenti, S., & Zerfass, A. (Eds.). (2016). *The management game of communication.* Bingley: Emerald Group Publishing Limited.

Carnegie, D. (1998). *How to win friends and influence people.* New York, NY: Pocket Books.

Carroll, C. E. (Ed.). (2013). *The handbook of communication and corporate reputation.* Malden, MA: Wiley-Blackwell.

Carroll, C. E. (Ed.). (2016). *The SAGE encyclopedia of corporate reputation.* Thousand Oaks, CA: SAGE Publications.

Charan, R. (2001). *What the CEO wants you to know: Using business acumen to understand how your company really works.* New York, NY: Crown Business.

Constable, S., & Wright, R. E. (2011). *The Wall Street Journal guide to the 50 economic indicators that really matter.* New York, NY: Harper Business.

Cope, K. (2012). *Seeing the big picture: Business acumen to build your credibility, career and company.* Austin, TX: Greenleaf Book Group Press.

Doorley, J., & Garcia, H. F. (2015). *Reputation management: The key to successful public relations and corporate communication* (3rd ed.). New York, NY: Routledge.

Freeman, R. E. (2010). *Strategic management: A stakeholder approach.* New York, NY: Cambridge University Press.

Goodman, M. B., & Hirsch, P. B. (2015). *Corporate communication: Critical business asset for strategic global change.* New York, NY: Peter Lang.

Grossman, D. (2012). *You can't not communicate: Proven communication solutions that power the Fortune 100* (2nd ed.). Chicago, IL: Little Brown Dog Publishing.

Grunig, L. A., Grunig, J. E., & Dozier, D. M. (2002). *Excellent public relations and effective organizations: A study of communication management in three countries.* Mahwah, NJ: Erlbaum.

Harrison, E. B., & Mühlberg, J. (2015). *Leadership communication: How leaders communicate and how communicators lead in today's global enterprise.* New York, NY: Business Expert Press.

Holtzhausen, D., & Zerfass, A. (Eds.). (2014). *The Routledge handbook of strategic communication.* New York, NY: Routledge.

Jones, R. W., & Kostyak, C. (Eds.). (2011). *Words from a page in history: The Arthur W. Page speech collection.* University Park, PA: The Arthur W. Page Center for Integrity in Public Communications, College of Communications, Pennsylvania State University.

Kaplan, R. S., & Norton, D. P. (2008). *Alignment: Using the balanced scorecard to create corporate synergies.* Cambridge, MA: Harvard Business Review Press.

Laskin, A. (Ed.). (2017). *The handbook of investor relations and financial communications.* Hoboken, NY: Wiley-Blackwell.

Leder, M. (2003). *Financial fine print: Uncovering a company's true value.* Hoboken, NJ: Wiley.

Lev, B. (2012). *Winning investors over: Surprising truths about honesty, earnings guidance and other ways to boost your stock price.* Boston, MA: Harvard Business Review Press.

Mackey, J., & Sisodia, R. (2014). *Conscious capitalism: Liberating the heroic spirit of business.* Boston, MA: Harvard Business Review Press.

Makoujy, R. J. (2010). *How to read a balance sheet: The bottom line on what you need to know about cash flow, assets, debt, equity profit...and how it all comes together.* New York, NY: McGraw-Hill.

Matha, B., & Boehm, M. (2008). *Beyond the babble: Leadership communication that drives results.* Hoboken, NJ: Wiley.

Men, R. L., & Bowen, S. A. (2017). *Excellence in internal communication management.* New York, NY: Business Expert Press.

Michaelson, D., & Stacks, D. W. (2017). *A professional and practitioner's guide to public relations research, measurement, and evaluation* (3rd ed.). New York, NY: Business Expert Press.

Miller, J. E. (2015). *The Chicago guide to writing about numbers: The effective presentation of quantitative information* (2nd ed.). Chicago, IL: University of Chicago Press.

Monks, R. A. G., & Minow, N. (2011). *Corporate governance* (5th ed.). Hoboken, NJ: Wiley.

Piper, M. (2013). *Accounting made simple: Accounting explained in 100 pages or less.* Lexington, KY: Simple Subjects, LLC.

Ragas, M. W., & Culp, R. (2014). *Business essentials for strategic communicators: Creating shared value for the organization and its stakeholders.* New York, NY: Palgrave Macmillan.

Roush, C. (2017). *Show me the money: Writing business and economics stories for mass communication* (3rd ed.). New York, NY: Routledge.

Roush, C., & Cloud, B. (2017). *The SABEW stylebook: 2,500 business and financial terms defined and rated* (3rd ed.). Portland, OR: Marion Street Press.

Skonieczny, M. (2012). *The basics of understanding financial statements.* Schaumburg, IL: Investment Publishing.

Slavin, S. (1999). *Economics: A self-teaching guide* (2nd ed.). New York, NY: Wiley.

Sowell, T. (2011). *Basic economics: A common sense guide to the economy*. New York, NY: Basic Books.

Stout, L. (2012). *The shareholder value myth: How putting shareholders first harms investors, corporations, and the public*. San Francisco, CA: Berrett-Koehler Publishers.

Taparia, J. (2004). *Understanding financial statements: A journalist's guide*. Portland, OR: Marion Street Press, Inc.

Tracy, J. A., & Tracy, T. C. (2014). *How to read a financial report: For managers, entrepreneurs, lenders, lawyers, and investors* (8th ed.). Hoboken, NJ: Wiley.

Wright, P. M., Boudreau, J. W., Pace, D. A., Sartain, E., McKinnon, P., & Antoine, R. L. (Eds.). (2011). *The chief HR officer: Defining the new role of human resource leaders*. San Francisco, CA: Jossey-Bass.

TRADE AND PROFESSIONAL ARTICLES RELATED TO BUSINESS ACUMEN

Cundick, D. (2015, February 6). 4 crucial PR skills you need (right now). PRNews Online. Retrieved from http://bit.ly/2oW5xeI . Accessed on April 22, 2017.

Czarnecki, S. (2016, November 9). Study: Comms head still struggles to gain CEO's favor. *PRWeek*. Retrieved from http://bit.ly/2pqG2Us. Accessed on April 22, 2017.

Duhé, S. (2013, December 12). *Teaching business as a second language*. Institute for Public Relations. Retrieved from http://bit.ly/1cGKcsw. Accessed on April 21, 2017.

Dupont, S. (2013, Winter). Understanding the language of economics is critical to communicating effectively. *The Public Relations Strategist*, 10−11.

Everse, G. (2011, August 22). Eight ways to communicate your strategy more effectively. *Harvard Business Review*. Retrieved from http://bit.ly/1wS2lRe. Accessed on April 24, 2017.

Feldman, B. (2016, November 28). Dear comms exec: Basic business skills are still required. *PR Week*. Retrieved from http://bit.ly/2ovUmWt. Accessed on April 20, 2017.

Friedman, M. (1970, September 13). The social responsibility of business is to increase its profits. *The New York Times Magazine*.

Friedman, M., Mackey, J., & Rodgers, T. J. (2005, October). Rethinking the social responsibility of business. *Reason*. Retrieved from http://bit.ly/3gxNgE

Kaplan, R. S., & Norton, D. P. (2004b, February). Measuring the strategic readiness of intangible assets. *Harvard Business Review*, *82*(2), 52–63.

Kaplan, R. S., & Norton, D. P. (2007, July–August). Using the balanced scorecard as a strategic management system. *Harvard Business Review*, *85*(7–8), 150–161.

Kolberg, B. (2014, March). Getting down to business at public relations agencies. *PR Update*, *49*(2), 6–7.

Lev, B. (2011). How to win investors over. *Harvard Business Review*, *89*(11), 53–62.

Phair, J. (2013, Winter). Developing a new generation of PR-savvy business leaders. *The Public Relations Strategist*, 28–29.

PRNews Pro. (2016a, August 29). PR pros still see writing as key to success, but analytics, digital, business skills also important. *PRNewsPro*, *7*, pp. 1, 3, 6.

PRNews Pro. (2016b, September 12). Report card from the academics: Next wave of PR pros lacks sharp writing, presentation skills. *PRNewsPro*, *7*, pp. 1, 3, 6.

Ragas, M. (2013, February 8). Require business 101 for every student. *The Chronicle of Higher Education*, *59*(22), A25.

Ragas, M. (2016). Public relations means business: Addressing the need for greater business acumen. *Journal of Integrated Marketing Communications*, *17*, 34.

Ragas, M., & Culp, R. (2013, Spring). Taking care of business: How PR pros and academics can build a stronger profession. *The Public Relations Strategist*, 15–16.

Ragas, M., & Culp, R. (2014, December, 22). *Public relations and business acumen: Closing the gap*. Institute for Public Relations. Retrieved from http://www.instituteforpr.org

Ragas, M., & Culp, R. (2015, May 1). Business weak: Five ways to build greater business acumen. *Public Relations Tactics*, 17.

Rockland, D. B. (2013, August 1). Learning to speak the C-suite's language. *Public Relations Tactics*. Retrieved from http://bit.ly/2oiMigQ. Accessed on April 23, 2017.

Sahel, J. (2017, February 14). The inner circle. *Briefings* (Korn Ferry Institute). Retrieved from http://www.kornferry.com/institute/the-inner-circle. Accessed on April 20, 2017.

Spangler, J. (2014, June 2). Valued communicators understand the business. Institute for Public Relations Research Conversations blog. Retrieved from http://bit.ly/1xiYB8n. Accessed on June 6, 2014.

WHITE PAPERS AND REPORTS RELATED TO BUSINESS ACUMEN

APCO Worldwide (2016, November). *Chief corporate communicator survey*. Chicago, IL: APCO Worldwide.

Arthur W. Page Society. (2007). *The authentic enterprise: An Arthur W. Page Society report*. New York, NY: Arthur W. Page Society.

Arthur W. Page Society. (2012). *Building belief: A new model for activating corporate character & authentic advocacy.* New York, NY: Arthur W. Page Society.

Arthur W. Page Society. (2013a). *Corporate character: How leading companies are defining, activating and aligning values.* New York, NY: Arthur W. Page Society.

Arthur W. Page Society. (2013b). *The CEO view: The impact of communications on corporate character in a 24×7 digital world.* New York, NY: Arthur W. Page Society.

Arthur W. Page Society. (2016, March). *The new CCO: Transforming enterprises in a changing world.* New York, NY: Arthur W. Page Society.

Arthur W. Page Society. (2017). *The Page principles.* Retrieved from http://www.awpagesociety.com/site/the-page-principles. Accessed on April 23, 2014.

Bain, M., & Jain, R. (2015, October). *Higher value through higher performance: Findings from quantitative research on talent development and management in communication.* Grand Rapids, MI: upper 90 consulting.

Bain, M., & Penning, T. (2017, March). *Understanding high performance in corporate communications functions today: Key insights from in-depth interviews with Chief Communications Officers.* Grand Rapids, MI: upper 90 consulting.

Byrum, K. (2013). *PRSA MBA program: Bridging the gap between strategic communications education and master of business administration (MBA) curriculum.* New York, NY: Public Relations Society of America.

Commission on Public Relations Education. (2012, October). *Standards for a master's degree in public relations: Educating for complexity.* New York, NY: The Commission on Public Relations Education.

Commission on Public Relations Education. (2015, May). *Summary report: Commission on Public Relations Education's (CPRE) industry-educator summit on public relations education.* New York, NY: The Commission on Public Relations Education.

FINRA Investor Education Foundation. (2016, December). *National financial capability study.* Washington, DC: FINRA Investor Education Foundation.

Library of Congress. (2011). *Financial literacy among retail investors in the United States.* Washington, DC: Federal Research Division, Library of Congress.

Marshall, R., Fowler, B., & Olson, N. (2015a). *The chief communications officer: Survey and finding among the Fortune 500.* Los Angeles, CA: The Korn Ferry Institute.

Marshall, R., Fowler, B., & Olson, N. (2015b). *Trusted counsel: CEOs expand C-suite mandate for best-in-class corporate affairs officers – and especially for the strategic advice they provide.* Los Angeles, CA: The Korn Ferry Institute.

Stacks, D. W., & Bowen, S. A. (Eds.). (2013). *Dictionary of public relations measurement and research* (3rd ed.). Gainesville, FL: Institute for Public Relations.

Swerling, J., Thorson, K., Tenderich, B., Yang, A., Li, Z., Gee, E., & Savastano, E. (2014). *GAP VIII:* Eighth communication and public relations generally accepted practices study. Los Angeles, CA: Strategic Communication & Public Relations Center, *Annenberg School for Communication and Journalism,* University of Southern California.

upper 90 consulting, & Holton Research. (2014). *Professional development in corporate communications today: Key insights from in-depth interviews with chief communications officers.* Grand Rapids, MI: upper 90 consulting.

USC Annenberg Center for Public Relations. (2017, March). *2017 global communications report*. Los Angeles, CA: USC Annenberg School for Communication and Journalism.

U.S. Securities and Exchange Commission. (2012, August). Study regarding financial literacy among investors. Washington, DC: Office of Investor Education and Advocacy, U.S. Securities and Exchange Commission.

Wright, D., Gaunt, R., Leggetter, B., Daniels, M., & Zerfass, A. (2009). *Global survey of communication measurement 2009 – Final report*. London: Benchpoint Ltd. and the International Association for Measurement and Evaluation of Communication (AMEC).

STRATEGIC COMMUNICATIONS-RELATED PROFESSIONAL AND ACADEMIC ASSOCIATIONS

Association for Education in Journalism and Mass Communication (AEJMC). Retreived from http://www.aejmc.org/

Association for Measurement and Evaluation of Communication (AMEC). Retreived from http://amecorg.com/

Business Marketing Association (BMA). Retreived from https://www.marketing.org/

Commission on Public Relations Education (CPRE). Retreived from http://www.commpred.org/

Financial Communications Society (FCS). Retreived from https://thefcs.org/

International Association of Business Communicators (IABC). Retreived from https://www.iabc.com/

International Communication Association (ICA). Retreived from https://www.icahdq.org/

International Public Relations Research Conference (IPRRC). Retreived from https://www.iprrc.org/

National Communication Association (NCA). Retreived from https://www.natcom.org/

Public Relations Society of America (PRSA). Retreived from http://www.prsa.org/

PR Council. Retreived from http://prcouncil.net/

PRSA Foundation. Retreived from http://www.prsafoundation.org/

National Investor Relations Institute (NIRI). Retreived from https://www.niri.org/

Society for Human Resource Management (SHRM). Retreived from https://www.shrm.org/

Society of American Business Editors and Writers (SABEW). Retreived from https://sabew.org/

UNIVERSITY-AFFILIATED STRATEGIC COMMUNICATIONS RESEARCH CENTERS

Arthur W. Page Center for Integrity in Public Communications. Retreived from http://comm.psu.edu/page-center

Corporate Communication International. Retreived from http://www.corporatecomm.org/

Donald W. Reynolds National Center for Business Journalism. Retreived from http://businessjournalism.org

Institute for Public Relations. Retreived from http://www.institute-forpr.org

Lillian Lodge Kopenhaver Center for the Advancement of Women in Communication. Retreived from http://carta.fiu.edu/kopenhavercenter/

The Museum of Public Relations. Retreived from http://www. prmuseum.org/

Plank Center for Leadership in Public Relations. Retreived from plankcenter.ua.edu/

USC Center for Public Relations. Retreived from annenberg.usc. edu/research/center-public-relations

FINANCIAL AND ECONOMIC LITERACY-RELATED WEBSITES

BusinessDictionary.com. Retreived from http://www. businessdictionary.com

360 degrees of Financial Literacy (American Institute of CPAs). Retreived from http://www.360financialliteracy.org/

Council for Economic Education (CEE). Retreived from http:// councilforeconed.org/

FINRA Investor Education Foundation. Retreived from http:// www.usfinancialcapability.org/

Investopedia. Retreived from www.investopedia.com

InvestorWords.com. Retreived from http://www. investorwords.com/

National Endowment for Financial Education. Retreived from http://nefe.org/

Securities and Exchange Commission (S.E.C.). Retreived from http://www.sec.gov

U.S. Financial Literacy and Education Commission. Retreived from https://www.mymoney.gov/

GLOSSARY

Accounting: The process of summarizing, analyzing, recording, and reporting business and financial transactions. Accounting is guided by detailed principles and procedures.

Accounts payable: A line on the balance sheet that is a liability, this figure is money the company owes to a supplier for a good or service purchased, but for which has not yet been paid.

Accounts receivable: A line on the balance sheet that is an asset, this figure is money owed to the company such as from the sale of a good or service for which funds have yet to be collected.

Adam Smith: A father of modern economics and the author of *The Wealth of Nations*, which argues that by operating out of self-interest individuals and firms inadvertently benefit others.

Advertising value equivalence (AVE): A controversial media metric that attempts to place a financial value on "earned" media coverage based on the cost to buy ad space in that publication.

Agency problem: Also known as "agency costs," this problem arises when the interests of an organization's board of directors and/or management diverge from that of stakeholders.

Agency theory: Theory that conceptualizes shareholders as the "principals" of an organization and the board of directors as the "agents" that act on behalf of shareholders in creating value.

Agenda-building theory: A theory that explores the role of organizational information subsidies in influencing how information is used and interpreted by influencers and stakeholders.

Agenda-setting theory: A theory that examines how the media's presentation of topics in the news over time focuses and shapes the public's perceptions of the world around them.

Al Golin: The founder of the global public relations firm GolinHarris and the originator of the "trust bank" concept in which companies build up deposits of goodwill through giving back.

Amortization: In corporate accounting, the deduction of capital expenses over the useful life of an intangible asset, such as a copyright, trademark, patent, or other intellectual property.

Analyst/investor day: A half- or full-day event held in a major city or at a company facility in which management provides the financial community with a detailed look at its business.

Analytics: A collection of numeric metrics or indicators that help track the performance of a communication campaign or program in meeting a stated objective or objectives.

Andrew Carnegie: Late 19th century industrialist and philanthropist who wrote the "Gospel of Wealth" in which he urged the wealthy to devote their resources to bettering society.

Annual meeting: A meeting held by a company typically after the end of its fiscal year. Many of these meetings are largely procedural with low in-person attendance, but there are exceptions.

Annual report: Document published annually that reviews the company's performance in the prior year. This document typically includes a letter from the CEO. May just be a 10-K wrap.

Applied research: Research that is conducted by or on behalf of an organization to solve a business challenge or address an opportunity. This research may be proprietary and non-public.

Arthur W. Page: Served as the vice president of public relations for AT&T. The first public relations executive to serve as an officer and member of the board of a major public company.

Arthur W. Page Center for Integrity in Public Communications: A research center at Penn State University dedicated to the study of ethics and responsibility in public communication.

Arthur W. Page Society: Based in New York and founded in 1983, a professional association for senior public relations and corporate communications executives with over 400 members.

Asset: A source of value for an organization. In a financial context, an asset is something that the organization owns or controls which is expected to contribute to the creation of future profits.

Association for Education in Journalism and Mass Communication: Founded in 1912, AEJMC is the largest association of journalism and mass communication educators and students.

Balanced scorecard: Strategic management approach popularized by Robert Kaplan and David Norton that gauges organizational performance using both financial and non-financial metrics.

Balance sheet: This document tracks a company's assets, liabilities, and net worth on an accounting basis. It summarizes what a company owns and owes at the stated period in time.

Bankruptcy: A legal process in which an organization restructures its financial obligations to creditors (known as a Chapter 11) or liquidates its assets and shuts down (known as a Chapter 7).

Baseline: Used in measurement and evaluation, a baseline is an initial measure of a campaign or program indicator that is used to assess future change in the performance of that indicator.

Basic research: Research that is conducted with the primary purpose of developing theory and contributing to the general body of knowledge. Academicians often conduct basic research.

Basis point: Also known as BPS, a basis point represents one 1/100th (0.01%) of 1.0%. A unit used to track percentage changes in interest rates and bond yields. A 100 BPS equals 1.0%.

Bear market: A market that is declining or expected to decline in value is said to be a "bear market." This phrase refers to the symbolism of a bear's claws pulling downward.

Bearish: An expression used to convey negativity about the overall stock market or a particular security. May also be used in a broader business context to convey negativity about something.

Behavioral economics: Sub-field of economics which studies the effect of emotional factors and the seemingly "irrational" economic decisions made by individuals and organizations.

Behavioral finance: Sub-field of finance which uses human and behavioral psychology to explain market behavior. Research in this field runs counter to the efficient market hypothesis.

Best practice: In a communication measurement context, a method or technique that has consistently demonstrated superior results compared to using other approaches.

Blackout period: The period around quarterly earnings reports in which company insiders cannot buy or sell shares of company stock. This limits the risk of insider trading charges.

Blue-chip company: A company with a high credit rating that has generated strong and predictable financial performance for years, if not decades, is said to be a "blue chip" company.

Board of directors: In a public company, the board of directors is elected by the company's shareholders and provides oversight and guidance to the company's senior management.

Bond: Generally considered safer than stocks, a bond is a form of debt that pays interest to the holder. Unless a convertible bond, a bond does *not* represent an ownership interest in a firm.

Book value: The stated net asset value of a company as carried on a company's accounting balance sheet (aka "the books"). Many intangible assets are not accounted for in this figure.

Bottom-line: Refers to an organization's net income. The name "bottom line" comes from the fact that net income is generally a line near the bottom of an organization's income statement.

Breakup fee: This is a fee that an acquiring company agrees to pay the to-be-acquired company if the transaction is not approved or the acquirer decides to back out of the agreement.

Bull market: A market that is rising or expected to rise in value is said to be a "bull market." This phrase refers to the symbolism of a bull thrusting its horns upward (i.e., a rising market).

Bullish: An expression used to convey optimism about the overall stock market or a particular security. May also be used in a broader business context to convey optimism about something.

Business Marketing Association (BMA): Founded in 1922, BMA is a national association of business-to-business (b-to-b) marketing and communications professionals.

Business model: A brief explanation of how a company intends to make money and create value for its stakeholders, and the factors that influence this value creation process.

C-suite: The C-level executives (e.g., CEO, president, CFO, CTO, CCO, and the like) that collectively make up the senior leadership team and top decision makers within an organization.

Capital: Money, property, and other assets of value that serve as the lifeblood of any organization. Investors provide capital to organizations with the goal of generating a profit.

Capital expenditure: Also known as "CapEx," funds spent on buying or improving fixed, physical, long-term assets such as property, plants, and equipment to generate future value.

Capitalized: Under accounting rules, an expenditure is capitalized if the item's useful life is believed to be longer than a year. Capitalized costs are amortized or depreciated over time.

Case study: A research approach that relies upon multiple sources of data to study a topic. This may include both quantitative and qualitative data sources as well as primary and secondary data.

Cash flow statement: This document literally "follows the money" and shows the amount of cash generated or spent by an organization in its course of business over the stated time period.

Cause marketing: A form of marketing in which a company partners with a non-profit organization and agrees to donate a portion of sales to the cause supported by the non-profit.

Cees van Riel: Leading scholar and consultant on corporate communication and reputation management. Co-founder and vice chairman of the Reputation Institute with Charles Fombrun.

Chairman: The chairman of the board serves as the leader of the organization's board of directors. The chair serves as a key conduit between the board and senior management.

Charles Fombrun: Leading scholar on corporate reputation, founded Reputation Institute and led the development of the Reputation Quotient® and RepTrak® corporate reputation measures.

Chief communication officer: A member of the C-suite, the CCO is tasked with managing the internal and external communications of the organization. Often serves as an advisor to the CEO.

Chief executive officer: The CEO is the top executive in an organization's C-suite, tasked with setting and implementing firm strategy. Often sits on the company's board of directors.

Chief financial officer: A member of the C-suite, the CFO is increasingly tasked with not just overseeing an organization's finances, but other executive level functions like firm strategy.

Chief operating officer: A member of the C-suite, the COO is tasked with the day-to-day management of an organization's operations. This person may also carry the title of president.

Classified board: For companies that have a classified or "staggered" board of directors, all directors do not come up for shareholder vote annually, but rather over a multi-year period.

Clawback provision: A provision included in an employment contract which allows the company to "clawback" previously paid compensation upon certain circumstances occurring.

Closely held: A closely held company refers to the fact that a company only has a small number of shareholders and is likely privately owned. The opposite would be a public company.

Commission on Public Relations Education: With representatives from 15 societies in PR and communication, the commission provides recommendations on standards in PR education.

Common stock: Security that represents an ownership interest in a firm and holds voting rights. In the event of a liquidation, creditors and preferred holders get paid before common holders.

Company insider: As defined by U.S. federal securities laws, company insiders are executive officers, members of the board of directors, large shareholders, and potentially outside advisors.

Consent solicitation: Some public companies allow corporate actions to be taken outside of the annual meeting format if a written consent solicitation receives majority shareholder support.

Consumer confidence: Survey-based measures of how the public feels about current and future economic performance. Consumer confidence can be predictive of future economic behavior.

Consumer Price Index (CPI): A popular gauge of the rate of inflation. The U.S. CPI measures changes in the average value of a basket of goods and services purchased by urban households.

Content analysis: A research method that may be quantitative or qualitative depending upon the approach. The analysis of the frequency and contents of textual and image-based messages.

Corporate finance: Concerned with the raising and managing of funds (i.e., capital) with the goal of maximizing value for stakeholders, particularly shareholder and investor interests.

Corporate gadfly: Individual investor that attempts to affect change at public companies. Pioneering gadflies have included the Gilbert brothers and Evelyn Davis among others.

Corporate governance: The system of checks and balances that attempts to make boards of directors and management more accountable and better aligned with stakeholder interests.

Corporate reputation: An overall assessment of a company by its stakeholders using a company's various dimensions as the evaluative criteria. The *attitude* held towards a firm.

Corporate social responsibility: The voluntary actions taken by a company to fulfill perceived obligations to stakeholders that go beyond maximizing profits and following the law.

Cost of capital: A concept in corporate finance, cost of capital is the cost of obtaining funds to grow a business. Generally speaking, a lower cost of capital helps improve profitability.

Cost of goods sold: Also known as "COGS" or "COS" (for cost of sales), these are the *direct* costs that go into producing a good or service. Indirect costs are excluded from this figure.

Council of Institutional Investors (CII): Founded in 1985, this association of investment funds with combined assets of $3 trillion dollars is a driving force in corporate governance.

Council of Public Relations Firms: With more than 100 public relations agencies as members, the Council advocates for and advances the business of public relations firms.

Credit: Entered on the right-hand side of an accounting ledger, a credit entry is made to record changes in value due to a business transaction. A debit is the opposite of a credit.

Cumulative voting: At some public companies, shareholders have the right to pool their votes all for one director nominee, thereby amplifying the voice of minority shareholders in elections.

Currency exchange rate: The rate at which one currency will be exchanged for another. Exchange rates fluctuate based on shifts in the economic conditions of the various countries.

Debit: Entered on the left-hand side of an accounting ledger, a debit entry is made to record changes in value due to a business transaction. A debit is the opposite of a credit.

Debt: A bond, loan note, mortgage, or other obligation, which states repayment terms on borrowed money and, if applicable, the interest owed as a condition of the borrowed money.

Declassified board: A board of directors in which all board of director seats come up for vote annually rather than a classified board where there is a staggering of terms for directors' seats.

Deflation: The opposite of inflation. Deflation is when prices for goods and services decline. Deflation leads to consumers delaying purchases and the value of assets declining.

Depreciation: In corporate accounting, the deduction of capital expenses over the useful life of a tangible asset, such as fixtures, equipment, vehicles, buildings and improvements.

Depreciation and amortization: Also known as "D&A," these related "non-cash" expenses on the income statement take into account the wear and tear of assets over the life of the asset.

Depression: A severe, long-term downturn in the economy. A depression is much worse than simply a recession. The most well-known U.S. depression is the Great Depression of the 1930s.

Depth interview: A qualitative research technique in which a researcher conducts a detailed interview with a subject one participant at a time. Also known as a one-on-one interview.

Diffusion of innovation theory: Theory that seeks to explain how, why and at what rate innovations are communicated through certain channels over time through a social system.

Disclosures: In an organizational and communication context, the release of organizational information that aids stakeholders in decision-making and reduces information asymmetry.

Dow Jones Industrial Average (DJIA): Often known as simply "the Dow," the DJIA is a widely followed stock market index comprised of 30 large, well-known U.S. companies.

Dual class stock: A type of ownership structure in place at some companies in which there are two or more classes of stock with one class having greater voting rights than the others.

Earnings: Terminology usually used with public companies, refers to the amount of money a company made or loss over a set time period. Earnings are the same at net income or net profits.

Earnings call: Generally held quarterly, a conference call at which company management discusses the company's latest financial performance and takes questions from investors.

Earnings guidance: Informational disclosures specifically focused on expectations about future company performance. The content of these forward-looking statements may vary widely.

Earnings per share (EPS): A measure of earnings or profits. Earnings per share is calculated by dividing the net income (i.e., net earnings) of a company by its number of shares outstanding.

Earnings release: A news release, typically distributed over a paid wire service, which reports the company's quarterly financial performance. The release may also include earnings guidance.

Economic cycle: Economies go through natural periods of growth followed by decline and then growth again. This process of expansion and contraction is known as an economic cycle.

Economics: The study of the cause-and-effect relationships in an economy. While often now housed and taught in business schools around the world, economics is actually a social science.

Economists: Study the consequences of decisions that people make about the use of land, labor, capital, and other resources that go into producing the products that are bought and sold.

Economy: The total aggregate sum of all goods and services produced among market participants. An economy may be studied at a local, regional, national or even international level.

EDGAR: All public company disclosure documents are required to be made with the U.S. S.E.C's EDGAR system. The full name is Electronic Data-Gathering, Analysis, and Retrieval.

Employment report: Regular reports, often issued by government agencies, providing data on the state of employment and the employment rate for a particular region, such as a country.

Enterprise value: This comprehensive valuation measure is the sum of the company's market capitalization (common stock) plus debt, any preferred stock and minority interest minus cash.

Environmental scanning: The process of monitoring the environment in which organizations and clients operate for issues, trends and other factors which may impact future decisions.

Environmental, social, governance (ESG): Refers to the various disclosures and policies that comprise an organization's environmental, societal, and governance impact on its stakeholders.

Equity: A stock or other security that represents an underlying ownership interest in a company. More broadly, equity refers to ownership in an asset after all debts have been paid.

Ethnography: Drawing from anthropology, a qualitative research technique in which the researcher observes, and potentially interacts with, participants in an area of their everyday lives.

Exchange traded fund (ETF): An investment fund that is bought and sold on an exchange like an individual stock, but which tracks the performance of a pool of securities or other assets.

Executive committee: A committee comprised of the members of the C-suite, as well as senior executives and division heads across the organization. Separate from the board of directors.

Exit, voice, loyalty: Framework developed by Albert Hirschman that explains how individuals will engage in either "exit" or "voice" when faced with declining quality in a relationship.

Expense: A cost that an organization incurs to generate revenue. This includes production, labor, leases, supplies, financing, and administration. Expenses are the opposite of revenue.

Expensed: Under accounting rules, an expenditure in which the total cost of the item is incurred all at once on the income statement. No amortization or depreciation is allowed.

Experimental design: A quantitative research method that relies upon the manipulation and control of variables in a laboratory-like setting to establish causation between variables.

Federal Open Market Committee (FOMC): An influential committee within the Federal Reserve System that makes decisions about monetary policy, including setting the fed funds rate.

Federal Reserve: Created in 1913 by the U.S. Congress, the Federal Reserve is the central bank of the United States. The Fed sets monetary policy with a goal of full employment and stable prices.

Fiduciary obligation: When referenced in the context of corporate governance, this refers to the legal duty that directors have to act in the best interest of the organization's stakeholders.

Financial Accounting Standards Board (FASB): An independent private organization which sets the generally accepted accounting principles (GAAP) for U.S. financial reporting.

Financial asset: Assets such as stocks, bonds, and cash that lack a physical embodiment, but are not considered intangibles since they basically represent claims on organizational assets.

Financial Communication Society (FCS): Founded in 1967, FCS is an association of financial services marketing and communication professionals. Chapters are in major financial centers.

Financial statements: Documents that state the financial health of an organization. The most well-known of these statements are the income statement, balance sheet and cash flow statement.

Fiscal year: The 12-month period that marks one full year of operations and financial reporting for an organization. Many organizations have a fiscal year that is the same as the calendar year.

Focus group: A qualitative research approach in which a moderator leads a semi-structured discussion with a group of participants that is recorded and then later analyzed.

Form 4: This document is required to be filed with the U.S. S.E.C.'s EDGAR system whenever there are changes in an insider's ownership (i.e., a purchase or sale) of company securities.

Form 8-K: This document is required to be filed with the U.S. S.E.C.'s EDGAR system whenever a material current event occurs in between a periodic report (i.e., 10-Qs and 10-K).

Form 10-K: This document is required to be filed with the U.S. S.E.C.'s EDGAR system. The 10-K reports a company's annual results and forms the foundation for a firm's annual report.

Form 10-Q: This document is required to be filed with the U.S. S.E.C.'s EDGAR system. The 10-Q reports a company's quarterly results. Unlike the 10-K, these financials are unaudited.

Form S-1: Also known as a prospectus, this registration document is required to be filed with the U.S. S.E.C.'s EDGAR system and is used by companies planning to go public.

FORTUNE Most Admired Companies: Launched by FORTUNE in 1982, this annual list was the first attempt at measuring and ranking the reputations of America's largest companies.

Forward-looking statement: A statement made by a company about future expectations and performance (i.e., guidance). Safe-harbor language should accompany such a statement.

Futures contract: A standardized agreement where both parties agree to buy and sell an asset, such as a physical commodity, of a specified quantity at a specified future date and price.

General and administrative expenses: Also known as "G&A," these are expenses related to the day-to-day operations of a firm rather than expenses related to the direct production of goods.

Generally Accepted Accounting Principles: Set by the Financial Accounting Standards Board (FASB), these principles help guide and provide consistency in U.S. financial reporting.

Glass, Lewis & Co.: Founded in 2003, this organization is a provider of proxy advisory services and shareholder voting recommendations to institutional investors.

Global Reporting Initiative (GRI): A non-profit organization that develops and promotes one of the most widely used sustainability reporting standards and frameworks for CSR reporting.

GMI Ratings: A research firm that provides advisory services to institutional investors on environmental, social, and governance-related (ESG) issues to help them manage risk.

Goal: A general statement rooted in the organization's mission and vision, stating what the organization intends to achieve; a goal tells stakeholders *"where* it is trying to go."

Golden handcuffs: Special incentives provided to top executives that encourage them to remain with a company and not to go to work for a competitor. Also called golden handshakes.

Golden parachute: An agreement, typically with a top executive, that the individual will receive certain significant benefits upon termination, often following a change in control.

Goodwill: In a corporate accounting context, an asset that is based on the amount paid for a company over its stated book value. This figure places a value on the acquired firm's intangibles.

Greenwashing: Derogatory term for when a company is perceived as spending more resources promoting and touting sustainable business practices than actually engaging in such behavior.

Gross Domestic Product (GDP): Widely followed economic indicator of a country or region's economic health. GDP represents the market value of all goods produced over a certain period.

Gross profit: Also called gross income, gross profit is a company's revenue minus its cost of goods sold. In other words, it is how much money is left over after deducting the direct expenses.

Guidance: The widespread practice of public companies attempting to improve transparency and manage investor expectations by releasing forecasts about future company performance.

Harold Burson: Called the most influential public relations leader of the 20th century, Burson is the founder of Burson-Marsteller, one of the world's largest communication agencies.

Harris Interactive: Best known for the Harris Poll on public opinion, this market research firm also co-developed the Harris Reputation Quotient (RQ)®, which is used in the reputation field.

Historical analysis: A qualitative research method that seeks to learn from and about the past through the collection and analysis of historical artifacts related to the topic of study.

Human capital: Term that recognizes that an organization's employees are a key source of future benefits. Human capital is typically viewed as a specific type of intangible asset.

Imperfect information: In an economics context, situations in which one party to a transaction has superior information than the other party, resulting in negative pricing and other actions.

Income statement: Also known as a profit & loss statement, this document tracks how much money an organization made or lost, and spent, on an accounting basis for the stated time period.

Independent director: Also known as an outside director, this is an individual who is not an employee of the company and does not have a material relationship with the company.

Individual investor: A small private, non-professional investor that typically buys small blocks of stock when making investments. Individual investors are sometimes known as retail investors.

Inflation: The opposite of deflation. Inflation is when the prices for goods and services increase. Inflation decreases the value of money and reduces its purchasing power.

Information asymmetry: A gap that occurs when one party to a potential transaction (i.e., the insider) is in possession of more and better information than the other party (i.e., the outsider).

Information intermediary: Any entity that reports, interprets, and analyzes information for broader consumption. In corporate finance, this includes financial journalists and analysts.

Information subsidy: Organizational communication vehicles and pre-packaged materials that lower the cost of information thereby increasing consumption by influencers and stakeholders.

Initial public offering (IPO): An IPO marks the first time that a company sells stock to the public and its shares are listed on a stock exchange and widely available for purchase.

Insider trading: The illegal practice of a company insider (i.e., executive or director), consultant or related party trading on and profiting from non-public, material information.

Institute for Public Relations: Located at the University of Florida and founded in 1956, this independent non-profit foundation is dedicated to the science beneath the art of public relations.

Institutional investor: A professional investor, such as a mutual fund, hedge fund, pension fund, or endowment, that typically buys large blocks of stock when making investments.

Institutional Shareholder Services (ISS): A subsidiary of MSCI Inc., ISS is a provider of proxy advisory services and shareholder voting recommendations to institutional investors.

Intangible asset: An asset that provides a source of future benefits, but lacks a direct physical embodiment. Examples include a firm's intellectual property, reputations, and relationships.

Integrated reporting: A "one report" approach to company reporting in which financial and non-financial performance metrics are presented in a format conducive to all stakeholders.

Intellectual property: A class of intangible assets that is generally the result of research and development (R&D) activities. This includes patents, trademarks, copyrights, and trade secrets.

Interest rate: The rate at which interest is paid by people or organizations to borrow money from lenders, such as banks. The Federal Reserve and other central banks impact interest rates.

International Accounting Standards Board (IASB): An independent body that is responsible for developing the International Financial Reporting Standards (IFRS) used around the world.

International Association for the Measurement and Evaluation of Communication (AMEC): Founded in London in 1996, AMEC is a global trade group that played a lead role in the establishment of The Barcelona Declaration of Measurement Principles and other standards.

International Association of Business Communicators (IABC): An association of approximately 15,000 business communication professionals based in over 80 countries.

International Communication Association (ICA): Founded in 1950, ICA is an academic association for communication scholars with more than 4,500 members in 80 countries.

International Financial Reporting Standards (IFRS): These accounting standards are overseen by the International Accounting Standards Board and used in more than 100 countries.

Investment bank: Financial organization that helps a company go public, sell stock or bonds, and advise it on financial transactions, such as mergers, acquisitions, or divestitures.

Investment conference: Typically organized by an investment bank, public companies are invited to make a presentation to professional investors and analysts. Often is webcast.

Investor relations: A strategic communication function in most public companies that serves as the primary interface between the financial community and company management.

Jawboning: The planned, purposeful use of statements by government actors, such as the Federal Reserve, to try to influence economic behavior and conditions in the financial markets.

Jumpstart Our Business Startups Act: Passed in 2012 and known as the JOBS Act, this legislation loosened securities regulations on smaller companies and helped promote growth.

Key performance indicator (KPI): A measure designed to gauge the performance of an organization or business unit at advancing or achieving a stated strategy, goal, or objective.

Lead director: Also called a "presiding director," the lead director presides over meetings of the independent directors of the board; this position's level of power varies by company.

Leveraged buyout (LBO): Typically associated with "going private" transactions and private equity firms. An LBO involves the use of a mix of debt and equity to acquire a company.

Liability: The opposite of an asset, a liability is an obligation that an organization takes on during the course of business, such as debt, accounts payable, or future incomes taxes payable.

Liquidity: A concept in corporate finance, liquidity is concerned with the ability to buy and sell a security, such as a stock, quickly and at a low cost with a limited effect on the market price.

Macroeconomics: Concerned with the study of the economy as a whole. Assesses the economy at a *macro-level* and studies the interactions of its various market participants.

Majority voting: In the context of board of director elections, majority voting stipulates a director must receive majority shareholder support or otherwise tender their resignation.

Management, Discussion & Analysis (MD&A): A section of a company's proxy statement in which management discusses the company's prior year performance and discusses future plans.

Market capitalization: Also known as "market cap," this valuation measure is calculated by multiplying the company stock price times the total number of shares of stock outstanding.

Market maker: Specialists that stand ready to buy and sell a particular stock on a regular basis at the publicly quoted price. Market makers are essential to the functioning of stock exchanges.

Market-to-book ratio: A valuation ratio calculated by taking a public company's total market capitalization and dividing it by the company's accounting book value (i.e., net asset value).

Materiality: In a public company context, information is considered material if a typical investor would likely view such information as important in affecting their investment decision.

Media clipping: Also known as a media placement or hit. The term goes back to when strategic communicators would "clip" articles and maintain records of media coverage in clip books.

Media impressions: The maximum size of an audience that might have been exposed to a communication message as the result of a placement. Based on the publication's circulation size.

Media placement: Also known as a hit or a clip. A placement is a news item or story that is attributed to strategic communication efforts, such as interactions with a journalist or influencer.

Metric: An informal term for a campaign or program measure or indicator. More specifically, a numeric value that should help determine whether a stated objective is being met.

Microeconomics: Concerned with the study of individual firms and households. Approaches economics from a *micro-level*, assessing the economic decisions of specific organizations.

Milton Friedman: A winner of the Nobel Prize in Economic Sciences, this free market economist is most closely associated with shareholder theory and shareholder primacy.

Mission: A brief description of why an organization exists and how it creates value for stakeholders. The organizational mission may be codified in a mission statement.

Mixed methods: A research approach in which multiple research techniques, specifically both quantitative methods and qualitative methods, are used to study and evaluate a topic of interest.

Multiple-step flow theory: Also known as the two-step flow theory, identifies the role of opinion leaders in the spread of information from the mass media to the general public.

Multipliers: The disputed notion that earned media coverage is worth more than or a "multiple of" paid advertising space in the same publication. Often used with ad value equivalencies.

NASDAQ: Founded in 1971, the NASDAQ is the second largest stock exchange in the United States and the world, behind only the NYSE. The NASDAQ is owned by the NASDAQ OMX Group.

National Investor Relations Institute (NIRI): Founded in 1969 and based in the United States, it is the world's largest professional association of corporate investor relations officers and consultants.

Need for orientation: Concept which finds that news media reporting has the greatest impact on shaping perceptions when people have high *relevance* and high *uncertainty* regarding a topic.

Negative equity: Also known as negative shareholders' equity, this occurs when total liabilities exceed total assets at a company. This indicates the firm may have trouble funding its operations.

Net income: Also known as net profit, net earnings or the "bottom line," this figure shows how much money a firm made after taking into account both operating and *non*-operating expenses.

Net margin: A ratio of profitability calculated as net income or net profit divided by *all* expenses (both operating- and non-operating expenses, such as interest and taxes).

New York Stock Exchange: Also known as "the Big Board," the NYSE is the oldest and largest stock exchange in the world. The NYSE is operated by NYSE Euronext.

Non-deal road show: A series of meetings held in various financial center cities in which company management meets with current and prospective large shareholders.

Non-financial information: Information that companies are generally not required to disclose, but which provides insights into the management and performance of intangible assets.

Non-governmental organization (NGO): An organization that operates independently of government and has a mission committed to advancing environmental or social issues.

Non-organic growth: In a business context, "non-organic" refers to business growth that is generated through acquisitions rather than through ownership of existing business operations.

Non-random sample: A sample in which every member of a target population *does not* have an equal chance of being selected. Also known as a non-probability sample.

Objectives: Specific statements emerging from a goal presented in clear, measurable, realistic, and time-bounded terms; tells us "how we will know *if* and *when* we have gotten there."

Open outcry: Also called pit trading, this form of trading relies on verbal bids, offers, and hand signals, unlike electronic trading which is fully computerized. The NYSE still has open outcry.

Operating income: Also called operating profit or income from operations, this figure shows how much money a firm made or lost after taking into account all of its operating expenses.

Operating margin: A ratio of profitability calculated as operating income or operating profit divided by net revenue. This measure does not take into account non-operating expenses.

Options contract: A contract that offers the buyer the right — but not the obligation — to buy ("call") or sell ("put") a security at a specified future date and price during a certain time period.

Organic growth: In a business context, "organic" refers to growth that is generated internally via a company's existing operations rather than growth that comes through acquisitions.

Outcome: The most sophisticated level of evaluation; measures the establishment, change or reinforcement in stakeholders' opinions, attitudes, or behaviors based on campaign messages.

Output: The most basic level of evaluation; measures the distribution of and possible exposure to campaign messages by stakeholders. Media analysis of third party content falls under outputs.

Outtake: An intermediate level of evaluation; measures whether targeted stakeholders actually received, paid attention to, understood and/or or retained the campaign messages.

Over the counter (OTC): A security, such as a stock, that is available for purchase, but is not listed on a formal stock exchange. Stocks traded "over the counter" are usually of higher risk.

P&L: An informal name for a profit and loss statement. The P&L is simply another name for the income statement, which tracks a company's revenue and expenses on an accounting basis.

Page Up: Affiliated with the Arthur W. Page Society, this organization is for Page members' most senior staff leaders. It is committed to developing the next generation of CCOs.

Pink sheets: Originally a list of securities printed on sheets of pink paper, the securities quoted on the pink sheet system are not listed on a formal exchange and generally are speculative.

Plank Center for Leadership in Public Relations: Named after Betsy Plank, this center housed at The University of Alabama supports leadership in PR education and practice.

Poison pill: A type of anti-takeover provision, a poison pill limits the amount of stock that any one shareholder can own beyond a certain threshold, thereby giving more power to the board.

PR Return on Investment (PR ROI): The impact of a public relations program on business results. The outcome variable which demonstrates the impact of a PR investment on business.

Preferred stock: A special class of stock that has priority over common stock holders in the event of liquidation. Preferred shares generally have a fixed dividend, but no voting rights.

Private company: A private company is a company whose shares are *not* listed on a stock exchange and has a small number of shareholders. May also be called a closely held company.

Private equity firm: A type of professional investor that invests in large, more established companies using a mix of debt and equity. May hold ownership stakes in public companies.

Profit margin: A measure of operational efficiency which shows how much a company makes (i.e., earnings) on a percentage basis for each dollar of sales it generates after various expenses.

Property, plant, and equipment (PP&E): This line on the balance sheet records the estimated value of this broad category of physical assets, ranging from company real estate to equipment.

Prospectus: A legal document that offers for sale securities, such as stock in a company. The prospectus outlines the business, its financial performance, risks factors, and the use of funds.

Proxy adviser: A specialized investment research firm hired by institutional investors to advise them on how to vote on corporate ballot issues, such as elections for board of director seats.

Proxy contest: Also known as a proxy fight, such situation typically occurs when there is a contested election between a dissident investor and the company for one or more board seats.

Proxy solicitor: A specialized communication and research firm hired by public companies or large shareholders to predict and influence the voting outcomes on corporate ballot issues.

Proxy statement: Formally known as a DEF14A filing with the S.E.C., this governance-oriented document is distributed annually in advance of a public company's annual meeting.

Public company: A public company is a company whose shares are listed on a stock exchange and is widely available for purchase by the public. May also be called a listed company.

Public Relations Society of America (PRSA): With 21,000 members across the United States, it is the world's largest professional association for public relations and communication professionals.

Publicity Club of Chicago (PCC): Founded in 1941, it is the nation's largest independent public relations membership organization with a focus on Chicagoland and the Midwest.

Qualitative research: A general research approach that collects non-numeric textual or image-based data (i.e., soft data) from relatively small samples to uncover deep, rich insights.

Quantitative research: A general research approach that collects numeric data from random samples often with a goal of using statistics to generalize findings to a larger population.

Quiet period: As mandated by U.S. federal securities law, a company that has registered to sell stock (e.g., IPO) is limited in the public statements it can make. Many public companies also choose to voluntarily adopt "quiet periods" around the release of quarterly earnings.

R. Edward Freeman: Business philosopher that is most closely associated with stakeholder theory, the concept of stakeholders, and the moral responsibility the firm has to stakeholders.

Random sample: A sample in which every member of a target population has an equal chance of being selected. Also known as a probability sample. Statistics assume random samples.

Recession: A period of economic decline and contraction during an economic cycle. A recession is officially defined as two consecutive quarters (six months) of negative GDP growth.

Regulation Fair Disclosure: Also known as Reg FD, this federal regulation adopted by the S.E.C. in August 2000 promotes the full and fair disclosure of information by companies.

RepTrak®: Launched in 2005, an annual measure of corporate reputation designed by scholars Charles Fombrun and Cees van Riel of Reputation Institute, a research and consulting firm.

Reputation management: The strategic communication and actions taken by a company to manage its reputation an intangible asset that is co-owned by the company and its stakeholders.

Reputation Quotient (RQ)®: Launched in 1999, the RQ® is an annual measure of corporate reputation designed by scholar Charles Fombrun and market research firm Harris Interactive.

Research and development (R&D): An expense line on the income statements that tracks spending on the development of new products, processes, procedures or related innovations.

Retained earnings: Also known as retained profits or retained income. The profits left in an organization's bank accounts to invest back in the business after paying out any dividends.

Return on Expectations (ROE): A metric that assesses the combined impact of financial and non-financial variables on stakeholder expectations, which leads to public relations ROI.

Return on Investment (ROI): An indicator of net financial performance based on an ratio of how much profit or cost savings is realized from an activity against its actual cost.

Revenue: The amount of money received for the sale of a good. Also known as sales, revenue is referred to as the "top-line" since this figure appears near the top of the income statement.

Road show: A series of meetings held in financial centers in which a company's management team, investment bankers, and other advisors meet with prospective large shareholders.

Rule 14(a)8: A rule passed by the S.E.C. in 1943, which allowed shareholders for the first time to submit some shareholder proposals for inclusion in public company's proxy materials.

Russell 2000: A widely followed stock market index, the Russell 2000 is comprised of 2,000 small capitalization U.S. companies. This index is a key measure of "small cap" performance.

Safe harbor language: As part of the Securities Litigation Reform Act of 1995, firms may list current risk factors when making forward statements to protect against frivolous lawsuits.

Say-on-frequency: A provision in the Dodd–Frank Act of 2010 gives shareholders the right to cast an advisory vote on how frequently shareholders should vote on executive compensation.

Say-on-pay: A provision in the Dodd–Frank Act of 2010 gives shareholders the right to cast an advisory vote on executive compensation packages. This non-binding vote is known as say-on-pay.

Schedule 13D: A filing that is required to be made with the U.S. S.E.C.'s EDGAR system within ten days of whenever anyone acquires a more than 5% voting stake in a public company.

Schedule 13G: An alternative to the Schedule 13D, the 13G filing connotates that the investor tends to have only a passive (rather than active) ownership position in the public company.

Secondary offering: Occurs when an already public company decides to sell additional shares of stock in order to raise money for the company and/or allow company insiders to sell shares.

Securities: Financial instruments that represent some type of financial value such as an ownership interest in a company (stock) or money that is borrowed and must be repaid (bond).

Securities laws: The laws that govern the offer and sale of securities. This includes the mandatory and voluntary disclosure of material, non-public information to the market.

Selective disclosure: Illegal practice in which select market participants are made aware of material, non-public information about a public company ahead of the broader market.

Selling, general, and administrative (SG&A): Broad expense category line that appears on a company's income statement. Spending on strategic communication falls under SG&A.

Shareholder activism: Attempt by one or more company shareholders to affect change at an organization through a variety of strategies, ranging from private meetings to proxy contests.

Shareholder primacy: A perspective embedded in classic agency theory in which the board of directors first and foremost makes decisions based on how such actions affect shareholder value.

Shareholder proposal: A proposal submitted by a shareholder for inclusion in a public company's proxy statement. Votes on shareholder proposals are typically advisory/non-binding.

Shareholder theory: Most closely associated with economist Milton Friedman, this theory posits that a company should maximize profits for shareholders, while following the rules.

Shareholders' equity: Also known as net worth or book value, this line on the balance sheet is equal to total assets minus total liabilities. This is share capital invested plus retained earnings.

Shares outstanding: Shown on a company's balance sheet, this figure represents the total number of shares currently outstanding and owned by shareholders, including insiders.

Signaling theory: A theory into the process of how and why market participants engage in costly and observable behaviors, known as "signals," which reduce information asymmetry.

Socially responsible companies (SRC): Moving beyond corporate social responsibility (CSR) initiatives and programs towards embedding CSR into the very core of a firm's business model.

Sovereign wealth fund (SWF): A government owned investment fund or entity that is funded by a country's foreign currency reserves. These funds invest in securities and other assets.

Special meeting: When a major corporate event occurs, such as a pending merger or acquisition, a special meeting of shareholders may be called before the next annual meeting.

Spin-off: In a corporate context, refers to when a company separates off one or more of its operating units into a newly established standalone business. This is also known as a "spin-out."

Staggered board: A board of directors is said to be "staggered" when board seats come up for vote over a multi-year period rather than all seats coming up for vote on an annual basis.

Stakeholder: Individuals or groups that have a shared interest or "stake" in the performance of an organization. This includes customers, employees, suppliers, investors, and the community.

Stakeholder theory: Most closely associated with business ethicist R. Edward Freeman, this theory posits that firms have a responsibility to all stakeholder groups, not just shareholders.

Standard: In a communication measurement context, an agreed upon approach, process or idea used as a norm or model that facilitates comparative evaluations against and across campaigns.

Standard & Poor's 500 (S&P 500): A widely followed broad measure of the U.S. market, the S&P 500 stock market index is comprised of 500 large capitalization or "large cap" companies.

Statistics: A field of mathematics concerned with the collection and analysis of numeric data, often for purposes of making inferences from a sample data set onto the population of study.

Stock: A security that represents an ownership interest in a company and its future earnings. The two main classes of stock are common stock and preferred stock.

Stock exchange: A market where securities, such as shares of stock in a company, are bought and sold. A company must meet listing requirements to have its stock listed on an exchange.

Stock index: A collection of stocks that represent the change in value of a particular industry, sector or the overall stock market. The DJIA and S&P 500 are widely tracked indexes.

Stock option: An instrument that gives someone, whether a company employee or an investor, the right to buy a specific number of shares of stock at a particular price on a future date.

Stock split: An action in which a company divides its existing shares outstanding into additional shares. A stock split in itself does not change the total dollar value of the company.

Stock ticker symbol: In the U.S. market, a series of unique letters (or single letter) used to identify the publicly traded stock of a company. Goes back to the days of ticker tape machines.

Strategic communication: The purposeful use of communication to advance an organization's mission. Strategic communicators employ persuasion, relational, and informational approaches.

Strategy: An overall plan or method employed to achieve an organizational goal; not to be confused with *tactics*, which are specific elements implemented in support of a strategy.

Supermajority voting: In the context of corporate governance, a provision that states that proposed bylaw amendments must receive a high percentage (67% or greater) of total votes.

Supply-and-demand: A core tenet of economic theory and the pricing of goods and services. In a free market environment, shifts in supply and demand play a key role in affecting prices.

Survey: A quantitative research method that uses a standard series of questions to collect data from respondents to gauge the sample and/or population's beliefs, attitudes, and/or behaviors.

Sustainability: In a corporate context, refers to business practices and performance that meet current needs, while not compromising the environment and society for future generations.

Sustainability reporting frameworks: Standards developed by non-profit organizations to guide company sustainability reporting practices so that they are comparable across firms.

Tangible asset: An asset that has a direct physical embodiment such as real estate, factories and fixtures, equipment, vehicles, or product inventory. Also known as "hard" assets.

The Barcelona Principles: A set of seven measurement principles agreed to at a meeting of communication measurement and evaluation experts held in Barcelona, Spain in summer 2010.

The Dodd-Frank Wall Street Reform and Consumer Protection: Passed in 2010 in the wake of taxpayer-funded bailouts of Wall Street, this landmark legislation tightens and places new regulations over corporations, particularly those operating in the financial services sector.

The Great Depression: Severe worldwide economic depression that started in 1930 for at least a decade. In the United States, the Great Depression sparked the first wave of federal securities laws.

The Sarbanes–Oxley Act: Nicknamed "SOX" or "SarbOx," this U.S. federal accounting reform and investor protection legislation was passed in 2002 in response to corporate scandals.

The Securities Act of 1933: Also known as the Truth in Securities Act, this U.S. federal legislation regulates the offer and sale of securities. The Act promoted better disclosures.

The Securities Exchange Act of 1934: This landmark U.S. legislation governs the secondary trading of securities. The Securities and Exchange Commission was formed through this Act.

Third-party endorsement: Recommendation, verification, or similar action provided by a seemingly independent, objective third-party, whether the news media or another influencer.

Top-line: Refers to an organization's revenue or sales. The name "top line" comes from the fact that revenue is generally the first line at the top of an organization's income statement.

Transparency: In a communication context, the proactive efforts taken by an organization to be open, visible, and accessible to stakeholders about organizational policies and actions.

Triple bottom-line: A core concept of corporate social responsibility; companies have a responsibility to profits, people, and the planet rather than solely the traditional bottom-line.

Trust Barometer: An annual global survey conducted by public relations firm Edelman into the concept of trust by country on institutions, industry sectors, and informational sources.

Underwriter: An investment bank that is responsible for the distribution, pricing, and sale of securities by a company, such as during an initial public offering of a company's stock.

Unemployment rate: A percentage calculated from employment report data, which represents the ratio of unemployed people looking for work versus those that are currently employed.

USC Center for Public Relations: Housed at the University of Southern California (USC), the center seeks to bridge the gap between the PR profession and academia.

U.S. Securities and Exchange Commission (S.E.C.): U.S. federal government agency tasked with enforcing federal securities laws and regulating the securities industries and stock market.

Values: In an organizational context, these are the guiding ethical ideals and principles that an organization holds as important. Should guide the organization's mission and vision.

Venture capital firm: A type of professional investor that typically invests in private, fast-growing companies. Venture capital firms are often investors in pre-IPO companies.

Vesting period: In the context of corporate finance, refers to the time that an employee must wait until they are able to exercise stock incentives. Vesting encourages loyalty by employees.

Vision: The core tenets and values driving what an organization hopes to become and achieve.

Wall Street: A street in Lower Manhattan that is the heart of New York's financial district. Wall Street or simply "the street" is used to refer to the U.S. financial industry as a whole.

Warrant: Similar to an option, only that a warrant is a longer-dated instrument that gives the holder the right to purchase a security, usually a stock, at a specific price within a certain time.

Warren Buffett: Known as "the Oracle of Omaha," Buffett, the CEO of Berkshire-Hathaway, is regarded as one of the greatest investors of the century; also co-created "The Giving Pledge."

Written consent: In the context of corporate governance, written consent allows shareholders to take various corporate actions without having to wait for voting at the next annual meeting.

INDEX